The Complete Miniature Rose Handbook

Simple Steps to Grow and Care For Beautiful Mini Roses in Any Space

Comprehensive Strategies, Practical Advice, and Step-by-Step Instructions for Thriving Miniature Rose Gardens!

DID YOU KNOW

> Miniature roses are small, bushy plants that typically grow between 6 and 24 inches tall, making them perfect for limited spaces.

Table of Contents

Introduction
    The Beauty of Miniature Roses 1
    Why Choose Miniature Roses? 3
    About This Book 6

Chapter 1: Getting Started with Miniature Roses
    What Are Miniature Roses? 9
    Understanding Different Varieties 11
    Selecting the Right Miniature Roses for Your Space 14

Chapter 2: Preparing Your Garden Space
    Choosing the Best Location 17
    Soil Preparation and pH Levels 19
    Essential Tools and Materials 22

Chapter 3: Planting Miniature Roses
    When to Plant Miniature Roses 25
    Step-by-Step Planting Guide 27
    Initial Watering and Care 29

Chapter 4: Daily Care and Maintenance
    Watering Schedule and Techniques 33
    Fertilizing Your Miniature Roses 35
    Pruning and Deadheading for Continuous Blooms 38

Chapter 5: Container Gardening with Miniature Roses
    Choosing the Right Containers 41
    Soil Mixes for Potted Miniature Roses 44
    Tips for Indoor and Balcony Gardening 46

Chapter 6: Dealing with Pests and Diseases
    Common Pests and How to Identify Them 49
    Disease Prevention and Treatment 51
    Organic vs. Chemical Solutions 53

Chapter 7: Advanced Growing Techniques

Propagating Miniature Roses 56

Grafting and Budding Techniques 58

Creating Bonsai Roses 61

Chapter 8: Seasonal Care Routines

Spring: Preparing for Growth 64

Summer: Maintaining Health and Vigour 66

Autumn: Preparing for Dormancy 69

Winter: Protecting Your Roses 71

Chapter 9: Designing with Miniature Roses

Creating Stunning Rose Displays 74

Integrating Miniature Roses in Mixed Borders 76

Using Miniature Roses in Floral Arrangements 79

Chapter 10: Troubleshooting Common Issues

Yellowing Leaves and Their Causes 82

Poor Bloom Production 84

Addressing Wilting and Drooping 86

Chapter 11: Enhancing Bloom Quality and Longevity

Techniques for Bigger Blooms 89

Extending Blooming Period 91

Using Growth Regulators 93

Chapter 12: Water Management

Efficient Watering Systems 96

Mulching for Moisture Retention 98

Recognizing Water Stress 100

Chapter 13: Soil Health and Fertility

Organic Soil Amendments 103

Composting Tips 104

Soil Testing and Analysis 107

Chapter 14: Companion Planting and Biodiversity

Beneficial Companion Plants 110

Creating a Balanced Ecosystem 112

Pest-Repellent Plants 114

Chapter 15: Sustainable and Eco-Friendly Practices

Reducing Chemical Use 117

Water Conservation Techniques 119

Encouraging Wildlife 121

Chapter 16: Additional Chapter

Essential Terms Every Rose Gardener Should Know 124

Troubleshooting List 124

Miniature Rose Care Checklist 126

Conclusion 129

How to Grow and Care for
Miniature Rose

Introduction

The Beauty of Miniature Roses

Miniature roses captivate with their delicate, perfectly formed blooms and an array of vibrant colors. Unlike their larger counterparts, these petite plants offer an abundance of blossoms on compact bushes, making them ideal for small spaces and container gardening. Their exquisite flowers often mirror those of standard roses but on a smaller scale, delivering the same elegance and charm without requiring a vast garden. The versatility of miniature roses allows them to enhance various settings, from window boxes to urban balconies, bringing the beauty of roses to places where space is a premium.

The fragrance of many miniature roses is another compelling attribute, with scents ranging from subtle and sweet to rich and intoxicating. This sensory delight adds another layer of enjoyment to growing these plants, as their aroma can transform any space into a fragrant oasis. Miniature roses are not just visually appealing but also engage the senses, creating a multi-dimensional gardening experience. Their ability to thrive in various climates and conditions further enhances their beauty, as they can be cultivated almost anywhere with the right care.

Miniature roses come in a variety of forms, including single blooms, clusters, and even trailing varieties suitable for hanging baskets. This diversity allows gardeners to experiment with different arrangements and displays, making each planting unique. The variety in bloom shapes and colors ensures that there is a miniature rose to suit every taste and garden style. From classic reds and pinks to vibrant yellows and pure whites, these roses offer a spectrum of hues that can complement any garden palette.

Miniature Rose come in an array of vibrant colors, including classic shades like red, pink, yellow, orange, and white, as well as multicolored blooms

The hardy nature of miniature roses adds to their appeal, as they often require less maintenance than traditional rose bushes. Their smaller size means they are less prone to the common problems that afflict larger rose varieties, such as black spot and mildew. This resilience makes them a perfect choice for both novice gardeners and experienced horticulturists looking for a low-maintenance yet beautiful addition to their garden. Their compact size also means they can be easily moved and rearranged, allowing for greater flexibility in garden design.

The longevity of miniature roses is another reason for their popularity. With proper care, these roses can bloom repeatedly throughout the growing season, providing continuous color and interest. Their ability to flower from spring to fall ensures that they remain a focal point in the garden for much of the year. This extended blooming period, combined with their ease of care, makes miniature roses a worthwhile investment for any garden. The joy of seeing new blooms emerge regularly keeps the gardening experience fresh and exciting.

Miniature roses also make excellent gifts, symbolizing love, appreciation, and friendship. Their small size makes them easy to transport and present, while their beauty and fragrance leave a lasting impression. Whether given as a potted plant or as part of a floral arrangement, miniature roses convey a message of elegance and thoughtfulness. Their enduring blooms ensure that the recipient can enjoy their beauty long after the initial gift, making them a meaningful and lasting token of affection.

Cultivating miniature roses can be a rewarding hobby, offering both aesthetic and therapeutic benefits. The process of nurturing these delicate plants, watching them grow and bloom, provides a sense of accomplishment and joy. Gardening with miniature roses encourages mindfulness and relaxation, as the gardener becomes attuned to the needs and rhythms of the plants. The beauty of miniature roses lies not only in their physical appearance but also in the satisfaction and tranquility they bring to those who care for them.

Why Choose Miniature Roses?

Miniature roses are an excellent choice for gardeners of all skill levels due to their manageable size and relatively simple care requirements. Their compact form makes them ideal for small gardens, patios, and indoor spaces, providing flexibility for those with limited gardening areas. They are perfect for urban dwellers who want to bring a touch of nature into their homes without the need for extensive garden space. The ability to grow miniature roses in containers means they can be moved indoors during harsh weather, protecting them from the elements and extending their growing season.

The adaptability of miniature roses to various growing conditions is another compelling reason to choose them. They can thrive in both full sun and partial shade, making them suitable for a range of environments. This versatility allows gardeners to experiment with different placements and arrangements, enhancing the visual appeal of their gardens. Miniature roses can also tolerate a variety of soil types, provided they are well-draining, which further broadens their suitability for different gardening situations.

Miniature roses offer a long blooming season, often flowering from spring through fall, which ensures continuous color and interest in the garden. Their frequent blooming cycle is a significant advantage for gardeners seeking year-round beauty. This extended period of bloom, combined with the plant's compact size, makes miniature roses an ideal choice for creating vibrant and dynamic garden displays. Their ability to produce numerous blooms on a small bush maximizes the visual impact within a limited space.

The low maintenance requirements of miniature roses are particularly appealing to busy gardeners. These plants typically require less pruning and pest management compared to larger rose varieties. Their resilience to common rose diseases reduces the need for frequent treatments, making them a practical choice for those who prefer a low-effort yet rewarding gardening experience. The ease of care associated with miniature roses makes them an excellent option for beginners looking to develop their gardening skills without being overwhelmed.

Miniature roses are also an economical choice for gardeners. Their smaller size means they often cost less than larger rose bushes, making it affordable to purchase several varieties and create diverse displays. The reduced need for extensive fertilizers and pesticides further lowers the cost of maintenance. This affordability, coupled with their enduring beauty and long blooming period, offers great value for money. Investing in miniature roses allows gardeners to enjoy the aesthetic benefits of roses without the high costs associated with traditional rose cultivation.

The compact size of miniature roses makes them perfect for creative gardening projects. They can be used to create stunning focal points in small spaces, such as window boxes, hanging baskets, or tabletop gardens. Their versatility allows for innovative designs and arrangements, providing endless possibilities for garden creativity. Miniature roses can also be incorporated into larger garden landscapes as accents, adding bursts of color and interest among other plants. Their adaptability to different garden styles makes them a versatile addition to any gardening repertoire.

Growing miniature roses can also have environmental benefits. By choosing to grow these plants, gardeners contribute to the biodiversity of their local area, providing habitat and food sources for pollinators such as bees and butterflies. The small size of miniature roses means they require less water and fewer resources, making them a more sustainable option compared to larger, more demanding plants. This ecological advantage, combined with their beauty and ease of care, makes miniature roses an attractive choice for environmentally conscious gardeners.

About This Book

This book is designed to be a comprehensive guide for anyone interested in growing and caring for miniature roses. Whether a seasoned gardener or a complete novice, readers will find valuable information and practical advice to help them succeed. The aim is to demystify the process of cultivating these charming plants, breaking down each step into manageable and understandable sections. By providing clear, concise instructions and expert tips, this book seeks to empower readers to create beautiful and thriving miniature rose gardens in any space.

Each chapter delves deeply into specific aspects of miniature rose care, from selecting the right varieties to advanced growing techniques. The structured layout ensures that readers can easily find the information they need, whether they are just starting or looking to refine their gardening skills. Detailed subchapters cover every topic imaginable, providing a wealth of knowledge that is both accessible and thorough. This approach ensures that no stone is left unturned, offering a complete resource for miniature rose enthusiasts.

Practical advice is complemented by expert insights, drawn from years of experience in growing and cultivating miniature roses. These insights help to address common challenges and provide solutions that are both effective and easy to implement. By sharing tried-and-tested methods, this book aims to instill confidence in readers, enabling them to tackle any issues that may arise. The blend of practical tips and expert knowledge ensures that readers have all the tools they need to succeed.

Special chapters dedicated to a Glossary of Terms, Troubleshooting List, and Care Checklist provide additional support and resources. The Glossary of Terms clarifies important gardening terminology, ensuring readers fully understand the language of rose cultivation. The Troubleshooting List offers quick solutions to common problems, acting as a handy reference for when things go wrong. The Care Checklist outlines daily, weekly, monthly, and seasonal tasks, helping readers stay organized and on track with their rose care routines.

The book also emphasizes the joy and satisfaction that come from growing miniature roses. Beyond the practicalities, it explores the aesthetic and therapeutic benefits of gardening with these delightful plants. By fostering a deeper appreciation for miniature roses, the book aims to enhance the overall gardening experience. Readers are encouraged to take time to enjoy the beauty of their roses, finding moments of peace and relaxation amidst their busy lives. The emotional and psychological benefits of gardening are highlighted, underscoring the holistic value of this rewarding hobby.

Illustrations and photographs throughout the book provide visual guidance and inspiration. These images help to clarify instructions and showcase the beauty of miniature roses in various settings. By providing visual examples, the book makes it easier for readers to envision their own gardening projects and understand the potential of these versatile plants. The combination of text and visuals creates a rich and engaging learning experience, appealing to both the practical and creative aspects of gardening.

Overall, this book serves as a complete manual for anyone looking to grow and enjoy miniature roses. By covering every aspect of rose care in detail, it aims to be the definitive guide on the subject. Whether seeking to add a touch of beauty to a small space or looking to master the art of rose gardening, readers will find everything they need within these pages. The book's thorough and accessible approach ensures that growing miniature roses is a rewarding and enjoyable experience for everyone.

Chapter 1

Getting Started with Miniature Roses

What Are Miniature Roses?

Miniature roses have a compact size, perfect for small spaces.

Miniature roses are a delightful variety of the classic rose, distinguished by their smaller size and equally captivating beauty. These roses, which typically grow to a height of 6 to 24 inches, are known for their diminutive blooms that replicate the intricate form of full-sized roses. Despite their small stature, miniature roses are robust and capable of producing an abundance of flowers throughout their growing season. Their compact nature makes them an excellent choice for container gardening, small spaces, and decorative accents in larger garden settings.

The origins of miniature roses can be traced back to the early 18th century, when these charming plants were first developed in Europe. Through selective breeding, horticulturists have created a wide range of miniature roses, offering various colors, fragrances, and forms. Modern miniature roses are often hybrids of the Rosa chinensis, known for its ability to bloom repeatedly, and other species roses that contribute to their hardiness and diverse characteristics. This rich genetic background ensures that miniature roses are both beautiful and resilient, capable of thriving in a variety of climates and conditions.

Miniature roses exhibit the same growth habits and care requirements as their larger counterparts, making them a versatile addition to any garden. They produce blooms in clusters or singly, depending on the variety, and can flower continuously from spring through fall with proper care. The foliage of miniature roses is also smaller in scale, adding to the overall delicate appearance of the plant. This scale allows for intricate garden designs and combinations with other plants, creating a visually pleasing and harmonious landscape.

One of the most appealing aspects of miniature roses is their adaptability. These plants can be grown in traditional garden beds, containers, hanging baskets, and even as indoor plants with adequate light. Their small size and manageable growth habits make them suitable for urban gardening, where space is often limited. Miniature roses can also be used in bonsai culture, adding a unique and artistic element to this ancient gardening practice. The versatility of miniature roses makes them a favorite among gardeners of all skill levels.

The fragrance of miniature roses varies widely, from the subtle to the intensely aromatic, offering a sensory experience that enhances their visual appeal. Many varieties have been specifically bred for their scent, providing delightful olfactory pleasure in addition to their stunning appearance. This characteristic makes them a popular choice for floral arrangements and personal enjoyment in home gardens. The combination of beauty and fragrance ensures that miniature roses are a standout feature in any setting.

Caring for miniature roses involves many of the same practices as caring for larger roses, including proper watering, feeding, pruning, and pest management. Their smaller size, however, often means they are less susceptible to some of the common diseases that afflict larger rose varieties. This resilience, coupled with their prolific blooming habits, makes miniature roses an ideal choice for gardeners seeking a low-maintenance yet highly rewarding plant. With the right care, miniature roses can provide years of beauty and enjoyment.

Miniature roses are also valued for their symbolic meanings, often associated with love, gratitude, and admiration. Their compact and perfect blooms convey a sense of elegance and refinement, making them a thoughtful gift for various occasions. Whether presented as a potted plant or part of a floral arrangement, miniature roses offer a lasting reminder of affection and appreciation. Their enduring popularity is a testament to their charm and the joy they bring to gardeners and flower enthusiasts alike.

Understanding Different Varieties

Hybrid miniature roses are among the most popular

Miniature roses come in a wide array of varieties, each with its unique characteristics and appeal. **Hybrid miniatures**, for instance, are among the most popular, known for their vigorous growth and abundant blooming. These hybrids are often derived from crosses between miniature roses and larger rose varieties, resulting in plants that combine the best traits of both. Hybrid miniatures can produce blooms in a variety of shapes and sizes, from delicate single flowers to full, multi-petaled blooms.

Patio roses, another popular variety, are slightly larger than typical miniature roses but still maintain a compact and manageable size. They are ideal for container gardening and can be used to create striking displays on patios, balconies, and terraces. Patio roses are often more robust and disease-resistant, making them an excellent choice for gardeners who want the beauty of roses without the extensive maintenance. These roses typically produce larger blooms and have a longer blooming period, providing continuous color and interest throughout the growing season.

Micro-mini roses represent the smallest end of the spectrum, with blooms that are often no larger than a dime. These tiny wonders are perfect for small spaces, rock gardens, and as accents in larger plantings. Despite their size, micro-mini roses are hardy and can produce a surprising number of blooms. Their diminutive stature makes them ideal for intricate garden designs and miniature landscapes, where they can be combined with other small-scale plants to create a cohesive and charming display.

Climbing miniature roses are another intriguing variety, offering the ability to cover trellises, fences, and other structures with their sprawling growth habits. These roses combine the compact blooms of miniatures with the vigorous climbing ability of larger roses, making them a versatile addition to vertical garden spaces. Climbing miniature roses can add height and dimension to a garden, creating lush, colorful backdrops and focal points. Their ability to grow vertically makes them ideal for maximizing space in smaller gardens.

Ground cover miniature roses are designed to spread and cover large areas with their low-growing, sprawling habits. These roses are perfect for creating colorful ground cover in garden beds, along pathways, and in border plantings. Ground cover roses are typically very hardy and disease-resistant, requiring minimal maintenance once established. Their ability to cover large areas with continuous blooms makes them a valuable addition to any garden landscape, providing both beauty and practical ground coverage.

The variety in bloom colors and forms among miniature roses is another aspect that enhances their appeal. From classic reds and pinks to vibrant yellows, oranges, and even bi-colored blooms, there is a miniature rose to suit every taste and garden design. Some varieties feature unique patterns and markings, adding an extra layer of interest and complexity to their appearance. The range of options allows gardeners to experiment with different color schemes and combinations, creating personalized and stunning garden displays.

Miniature roses also differ in their fragrance profiles, with some varieties bred specifically for their scent. The olfactory experience of growing fragrant miniature roses adds another dimension to their enjoyment, making them a sensory delight in the garden. Whether choosing a rose for its visual appeal, fragrance, or both, the diversity among miniature rose varieties ensures that there is a perfect plant for every gardener's preference. This rich variety offers endless possibilities for creating beautiful and personalized garden spaces.

Selecting the Right Miniature Roses for Your Space

Choosing the right miniature roses for a specific space involves considering several factors, including climate, available space, and personal preferences. Climate plays a crucial role in determining which varieties will thrive, as some miniature roses are more tolerant of heat, cold, or humidity than others. It is important to select varieties that are suited to the local climate conditions to ensure healthy growth and prolific blooming. Consulting with local nurseries and experienced gardeners can provide valuable insights into which miniature roses are best suited for a particular region.

Available space is another key consideration when selecting miniature roses. For small gardens, balconies, or indoor spaces, compact varieties such as micro-mini roses or patio roses are ideal choices. These roses can thrive in containers and small garden beds, providing vibrant color and beauty without overwhelming the space. For larger garden areas, climbing or ground cover miniature roses can add dimension and fill larger spaces effectively. Assessing the available space and choosing varieties that match the scale of the garden ensures a harmonious and visually pleasing result.

Personal preferences in terms of bloom color, form, and fragrance also play a significant role in the selection process. Miniature roses come in a wide range of colors, from classic reds and pinks to unique hues like lavender and peach. Some gardeners may prefer the traditional look of single-color blooms, while others might enjoy the complexity of bi-colored or patterned flowers. Fragrance is another important consideration, with some varieties offering strong, sweet scents that can enhance the sensory experience of the garden.

The intended use of the miniature roses should also be taken into account when making a selection. For example, if the goal is to create a colorful ground cover, varieties that spread and cover large areas would be ideal. If the roses are intended to adorn a patio or balcony, container-friendly varieties with a compact growth habit would be more suitable.

Understanding the purpose of the planting helps in selecting varieties that will perform well and meet the specific needs of the garden space.

Maintenance requirements are another factor to consider when choosing miniature roses. Some varieties are more disease-resistant and require less frequent pruning and care, making them ideal for gardeners seeking low-maintenance plants. Others may need more attention to keep them healthy and blooming. Considering the amount of time and effort available for garden maintenance helps in selecting varieties that align with the gardener's lifestyle and capabilities. Choosing low-maintenance varieties can make gardening a more enjoyable and stress-free experience.

Availability of light is a critical factor in the selection process, as miniature roses generally require a significant amount of sunlight to thrive. Assessing the light conditions in the garden and choosing varieties that match those conditions ensures healthy growth and abundant blooms. For areas with limited sunlight, selecting shade-tolerant varieties or considering supplemental lighting options can help in achieving the desired results. Matching the light requirements of the roses to the garden conditions is essential for their success.

Finally, it is important to consider the overall design and aesthetic of the garden when selecting miniature roses. The chosen varieties should complement the existing plants and structures, creating a cohesive and visually appealing landscape. Whether aiming for a formal garden with symmetrical plantings or a more casual, cottage-style garden with mixed borders, selecting varieties that fit the design theme enhances the overall look and feel of the garden.

Chapter 2

Preparing Your Garden Space

Choosing the Best Location

Miniature roses flourish in areas with plenty of sunlight.

Selecting the optimal location for planting miniature roses is a crucial step in ensuring their healthy growth and vibrant blooms. Miniature roses thrive in locations that receive ample sunlight, ideally six to eight hours of direct sunlight per day. This exposure is essential for photosynthesis, which fuels the plant's growth and flowering processes. A well-lit location also helps in reducing the risk of fungal diseases, which can be more prevalent in shaded, damp areas. Assessing the garden for the sunniest spots and planning the planting accordingly can significantly impact the success of growing miniature roses.

In addition to sunlight, the chosen location should have good air circulation. Proper airflow helps in preventing the build-up of moisture on the leaves, which can lead to fungal infections and other diseases. Avoiding areas that are prone to stagnant air or where plants are crowded together is important. Instead, opting for locations with sufficient space between plants ensures that air can move freely, keeping the foliage dry and healthy. Good air circulation is a key factor in maintaining the overall health of miniature roses.

The proximity to water sources is another consideration when choosing the planting location. Miniature roses require regular watering, especially during the growing season. Placing them near a convenient water source, such as a garden hose or irrigation system, makes it easier to maintain consistent watering schedules. This convenience helps in ensuring that the plants receive the necessary moisture without the gardener having to transport water over long distances. Ease of access to water is a practical aspect that can facilitate better care and maintenance of the roses.

The soil quality and drainage capabilities of the chosen location are also critical. Miniature roses prefer well-draining soil that prevents water from pooling around the roots, which can lead to root rot and other problems. Conducting a soil test to assess its drainage properties and amending it if necessary ensures a suitable growing environment. Adding organic matter, such as compost or well-rotted manure, can improve soil structure and fertility, providing a rich medium for the roses to thrive. Ensuring that the soil meets the needs of miniature roses is fundamental to their success.

Wind protection is an often-overlooked factor when selecting a planting location. While good air circulation is beneficial, exposure to strong winds can damage delicate rose blooms and foliage. Choosing a location that is sheltered from harsh winds, such as near a fence, wall, or hedge, can protect the plants while still allowing for adequate airflow. Windbreaks or temporary barriers can also be used to shield the roses from strong gusts, ensuring that they remain intact and healthy.

Considering the aesthetic placement within the garden is also important. Miniature roses can serve as beautiful focal points, edging plants, or accents in mixed borders. Planning their location in relation to other plants and garden features helps in creating a harmonious and visually pleasing landscape. Whether aiming for a formal arrangement or a more natural, informal layout, thoughtful placement enhances the overall design of the garden. Strategic positioning of miniature roses can elevate the garden's beauty and create stunning visual effects.

Seasonal considerations should also be taken into account when choosing the planting location. Understanding the microclimates within the garden, such as areas that receive more shade in winter or more sun in summer, can inform better placement decisions. Observing the garden throughout the year and noting how the light and weather conditions change can provide valuable insights. Adjusting the planting location based on these observations ensures that the miniature roses receive optimal growing conditions year-round, promoting their health and longevity.

Soil Preparation and pH Levels

Preparing the soil properly is a foundational step in growing healthy and productive miniature roses. The first aspect to consider is the soil texture and structure, which should be well-draining yet capable of retaining enough moisture for the plants. Sandy soils, which drain too quickly, can be amended with organic matter to improve water retention, while clay soils, which retain too much water, can be enhanced with sand and compost to improve drainage. Achieving the right balance ensures that the roots of the miniature roses receive adequate moisture without becoming waterlogged.

Conducting a soil pH test is essential in determining whether the soil is suitable for growing roses. Miniature roses prefer a slightly acidic to neutral pH range, typically between 6.0 and 6.5. Soil that is too acidic or too alkaline can inhibit nutrient uptake, leading to poor growth and reduced flowering. If the soil pH is not within the optimal range, it can be adjusted using appropriate amendments. For instance, adding lime can raise the pH of acidic soil, while sulfur can lower the pH of alkaline soil. Regular testing and adjustments ensure that the soil remains within the desired pH range.

Incorporating organic matter into the soil is a crucial step in enhancing its fertility and structure. Organic materials such as compost, well-rotted manure, and leaf mold add essential nutrients to the soil and improve its texture. These materials also promote beneficial microbial activity, which aids in breaking down organic matter and releasing nutrients that are readily available to the plants. Organic amendments not only enrich the soil but also improve its water-holding capacity and aeration, creating an ideal environment for the roots to thrive.

The process of soil preparation should also involve removing any debris, rocks, and weeds from the planting area. Clearing the soil of these obstructions ensures that the roots can grow freely and access the nutrients and water they need. Weeds, in particular, compete with roses for resources and can harbor pests and diseases. Thoroughly weeding the planting area and using mulch to suppress future weed growth helps in maintaining a clean and healthy growing environment. Preparing a clean and weed-free bed sets the stage for successful rose cultivation.

Improving soil drainage is another important aspect of soil preparation. Poor drainage can lead to waterlogged soil, which suffocates the roots and promotes root rot. Creating raised beds or mounds can enhance drainage by elevating the root zone above the surrounding soil level. Adding coarse sand or gravel to the planting area can also improve drainage by increasing the soil's porosity. Ensuring that excess water can easily escape from the root zone is essential for the health of miniature roses.

Fertilizing the soil before planting provides an initial nutrient boost that supports the young plants' growth. Using a balanced fertilizer that contains nitrogen, phosphorus, and potassium, along with trace elements, can enrich the soil and promote vigorous growth. Organic fertilizers, such as bone meal, blood meal, and fish emulsion, offer a slow-release source of nutrients that sustain the plants over time. Incorporating these fertilizers into the soil before planting ensures that the roses have access to the nutrients they need from the start.

Monitoring and maintaining soil health is an ongoing process that continues throughout the growing season. Regularly adding organic matter, adjusting the pH as needed, and ensuring proper drainage are all part of a comprehensive soil management strategy. Observing the plants and responding to any signs of nutrient deficiencies or poor growth helps in maintaining optimal soil conditions. By prioritizing soil health, gardeners can create a supportive environment that fosters the growth and beauty of miniature roses.

Essential Tools and Materials

Having the right tools and materials is essential for successful miniature rose gardening. Quality tools make the tasks of planting, pruning, watering, and maintaining roses easier and more efficient. A good pair of bypass pruners is one of the most important tools for any rose gardener. These pruners are designed to make clean cuts on live wood, which helps in promoting healthy growth and reducing the risk of disease. Regularly sharpening and cleaning the pruners ensures they remain effective and safe to use.

A sturdy garden trowel is another indispensable tool, useful for digging planting holes, transplanting roses, and adding soil amendments. Trowels with ergonomic handles provide comfort during extended use, reducing hand fatigue. Stainless steel trowels are durable and resistant to rust, making them a long-lasting addition to the gardener's toolkit. Having a reliable trowel ensures that planting and soil preparation tasks can be carried out efficiently and effectively.

Watering cans or hoses with adjustable nozzles are crucial for providing the roses with the right amount of water. Miniature roses require consistent moisture, and a watering can with a fine rose or a hose with a gentle spray setting helps in delivering water without damaging the delicate blooms and foliage. For larger gardens, drip irrigation systems can provide an efficient and automated way to water the roses, ensuring they receive consistent moisture while conserving water.

Mulch is an essential material for maintaining soil moisture and suppressing weeds. Organic mulches, such as bark chips, straw, or compost, decompose over time, adding valuable nutrients to the soil. Applying a layer of mulch around the base of the roses helps in retaining soil moisture, reducing temperature fluctuations, and preventing weed growth. Mulching is a simple yet effective practice that supports the health and vigor of miniature roses.

Fertilizers and soil amendments are also key materials for rose gardening. Balanced fertilizers that provide essential nutrients support the growth and blooming of the roses. Organic fertilizers, such as compost, manure, and bone meal, offer a slow-release source of nutrients that enhance soil fertility over time. Soil amendments, like lime or sulfur, are used to adjust soil pH, ensuring it falls within the optimal range for rose growth. Using the right fertilizers and amendments ensures that the roses have access to the nutrients they need to thrive.

Pest and disease control products are important for maintaining the health of miniature roses. Organic options, such as insecticidal soaps, neem oil, and beneficial insects, can effectively manage common pests without harming the environment. Fungicides may be necessary to prevent or treat fungal diseases that can affect roses. Selecting safe and effective pest and disease control products helps in protecting the roses from harm while minimizing environmental impact.

Protective gear, such as gardening gloves, knee pads, and sun protection, ensures the gardener's safety and comfort. Gloves protect the hands from thorns, cuts, and soil-borne pathogens, while knee pads provide cushioning for extended periods of kneeling. Wearing a hat and sunscreen protects against sunburn during outdoor gardening activities. Using the appropriate protective gear makes gardening more enjoyable and reduces the risk of injury.

In addition to these basic tools and materials, gardeners may find other items useful, such as garden markers for labeling rose varieties, stakes and ties for supporting climbing roses, and wheelbarrows for transporting soil and mulch. Organizing and maintaining these tools and materials ensures they are readily available when needed, making gardening tasks more efficient. A well-equipped gardener is prepared to care for miniature roses effectively, leading to beautiful and healthy plants.

Chapter 3

Planting Miniature Roses

When to Plant Miniature Roses

The timing for planting miniature roses is a crucial factor that influences their growth and flowering potential. The best period for planting depends largely on the climate of the region. In temperate climates, the ideal time to plant miniature roses is in the spring, after the last frost has passed and the soil has warmed up. This allows the roses to establish themselves during the growing season, benefiting from the milder weather and longer daylight hours. Spring planting provides ample time for the roses to develop strong roots before facing the stress of summer heat.

In regions with mild winters, fall planting can also be a successful strategy. Planting in the fall allows the roses to establish roots in the cooler, wetter conditions, which can be less stressful than the heat of summer. The key is to plant early enough in the fall to give the roses time to develop a healthy root system before the first frost. This strategy ensures that the plants are well-prepared to resume vigorous growth in the spring. Fall planting can result in stronger plants that are better equipped to handle the challenges of the growing season.

Container-grown miniature roses offer more flexibility in planting times compared to bare-root roses. Container-grown roses can be planted at almost any time of the year, provided the ground is not frozen or excessively wet. This flexibility makes container-grown roses a convenient option for gardeners who may miss the ideal spring or fall planting windows. However, it is still advisable to avoid planting during periods of extreme heat or drought, as these conditions can stress newly planted roses and hinder their establishment.

Understanding local climate patterns is essential for determining the best planting time. Consulting with local nurseries and experienced gardeners can provide valuable insights into the optimal planting schedule for specific regions. Additionally, paying attention to weather forecasts and soil conditions can help in making informed decisions about planting times. Proper timing sets the foundation for successful rose cultivation, ensuring that the plants have the best possible start.

The age and type of the rose plant also influence the planting schedule. Younger plants may be more susceptible to environmental stress and may require more favorable conditions to thrive. In contrast, established container-grown roses are typically more resilient and can handle a wider range of planting times. Assessing the specific needs of the roses being planted helps in choosing the most appropriate time to plant, maximizing their chances of success.

Planting during favorable weather conditions is another important consideration. Choosing a calm, overcast day for planting can reduce transplant shock and prevent the young plants from drying out. Excessive sun and wind can quickly dehydrate newly planted roses, making it harder for them to establish. Providing a sheltered, stable environment during the initial planting phase can significantly enhance the roses' ability to adapt and grow.

Timing the planting to coincide with favorable soil moisture levels is also beneficial. Soil that is too dry can stress the plants, while overly wet soil can lead to root rot. Ensuring that the soil is moist but well-drained creates an optimal environment for the roots to establish. Proper soil preparation and timing can create the ideal conditions for planting miniature roses, setting the stage for healthy growth and abundant blooms.

Step-by-Step Planting Guide

Planting Miniature Rose

Planting miniature roses requires careful preparation and attention to detail to ensure their successful establishment. The first step is to choose a suitable location that provides adequate sunlight and well-draining soil. Miniature roses thrive in locations that receive at least six hours of direct sunlight each day. Ensuring good air circulation around the planting area helps prevent disease and promotes healthy growth. Assessing the site and making any necessary adjustments to improve soil drainage or sunlight exposure sets the stage for successful planting.

Once the location is chosen, preparing the soil is the next crucial step. Begin by removing any weeds, rocks, or debris from the planting area. Loosen the soil to a depth of about 12 to 18 inches, incorporating organic matter such as compost or well-rotted manure. This enhances soil fertility and structure, providing a rich growing medium for the roses. Testing the soil pH and making adjustments as needed ensures that the soil falls within the optimal range of 6.0 to 6.5 for rose growth. Proper soil preparation creates a conducive environment for root development.

For bare-root roses, soaking the roots in water for several hours before planting helps rehydrate and prepare them for their new environment. Container-grown roses should be well-watered before planting to ease removal from the container and minimize root disturbance. Dig a planting hole that is wide and deep enough to accommodate the roots without crowding. For bare-root roses, create a small mound of soil at the bottom of the hole and spread the roots evenly over it. This encourages outward root growth and prevents the roots from becoming tangled or compressed.

Position the rose in the hole so that the graft union (the swollen area where the rose is grafted onto the rootstock) is at or slightly below ground level. This positioning helps protect the graft union from frost damage and encourages strong, stable growth. Backfill the hole with soil, gently firming it around the roots to eliminate air pockets. Water the rose thoroughly to settle the soil and provide initial moisture. Proper planting depth and soil contact are critical for the rose to establish itself successfully.

Applying a layer of mulch around the base of the rose helps retain soil moisture, regulate temperature, and suppress weeds. Organic mulches such as straw, wood chips, or compost are ideal choices. Avoid piling mulch directly against the stem, as this can lead to rot. Maintaining a mulch layer of 2 to 3 inches thick provides ongoing benefits throughout the growing season. Mulching not only aids in moisture retention but also contributes to soil fertility as it decomposes.

Staking or supporting the rose may be necessary, especially for taller varieties or in windy locations. Using soft ties, gently secure the rose to the stake, ensuring that it can move slightly with the wind. This flexibility helps strengthen the stem and prevents damage. Regularly check and adjust the ties as the rose grows to prevent constriction. Providing support helps the rose develop a strong, upright form and reduces the risk of wind damage.

Monitoring the newly planted rose closely during the initial weeks is essential for its establishment. Keep the soil consistently moist but not waterlogged, and protect the rose from extreme weather conditions if necessary. Applying a balanced fertilizer after the rose has started to grow can provide additional nutrients to support its development. Observing the plant for any signs of stress or disease and responding promptly ensures that the rose adapts well to its new environment and begins to thrive.

Initial Watering and Care

The first few weeks after planting are critical for the successful establishment of miniature roses. Consistent watering is essential to help the roses develop a strong root system. Newly planted roses should be watered thoroughly and regularly, keeping the soil evenly moist but not waterlogged. This initial watering helps settle the soil around the roots and provides the necessary moisture for root growth. Using a gentle watering method, such as a drip system or a watering can with a fine rose, ensures that the water is delivered effectively without disturbing the soil.

The frequency of watering depends on the weather conditions and soil type. In hot, dry weather, newly planted roses may need to be watered daily, while in cooler, wetter conditions, less frequent watering may be sufficient. It is important to monitor the soil moisture regularly and adjust the watering schedule accordingly. Overwatering can lead to root rot, while underwatering can stress the plant and hinder its establishment. Finding the right balance is key to supporting healthy root development.

Applying mulch around the base of the rose helps retain soil moisture and reduce the frequency of watering. Mulch acts as a barrier, preventing evaporation and keeping the soil temperature stable. Organic mulches, such as compost, straw, or wood chips, also add nutrients to the soil as they decompose. Maintaining a mulch layer of 2 to 3 inches thick is beneficial for moisture retention and weed suppression. Mulch not only supports the health of the roses but also reduces maintenance efforts for the gardener.

Protecting newly planted roses from extreme weather conditions is important during the initial establishment phase. In hot weather, providing temporary shade can help prevent heat stress and excessive evaporation. Shade cloths or temporary structures can be used to shield the roses from direct sun during the hottest part of the day. In windy conditions, creating windbreaks using garden screens or temporary barriers can protect the young plants from damage. Ensuring a stable, protected environment supports the roses' adaptation to their new location.

Fertilizing newly planted roses should be approached with care. While it is important to provide nutrients to support growth, applying too much fertilizer too soon can burn the roots and harm the plant. It is best to wait until the roses show signs of new growth before applying a balanced, slow-release fertilizer. Organic fertilizers, such as fish emulsion or compost tea, are gentle options that provide a steady supply of nutrients. Regularly monitoring the roses for signs of nutrient deficiencies helps in determining the appropriate fertilization schedule.

Pruning newly planted roses is generally not necessary during the initial establishment phase. However, removing any damaged or weak growth can help the plant focus its energy on developing a strong root system. As the roses begin to grow, light pruning can be done to shape the plant and encourage bushy, compact growth. Regular inspection and maintenance help ensure that the roses remain healthy and vigorous, setting the stage for robust flowering in the future.

Monitoring for pests and diseases is crucial during the early stages of establishment. Newly planted roses can be vulnerable to common rose pests, such as aphids, spider mites, and beetles. Regularly inspecting the plants and taking prompt action to address any infestations helps protect the young roses. Using organic pest control methods, such as insecticidal soaps or beneficial insects, can effectively manage pests without harming the environment. Ensuring that the roses remain healthy and pest-free supports their successful establishment and growth.

Chapter 4

Daily Care and Maintenance

Watering Schedule and Techniques

Establishing a consistent watering schedule is essential for maintaining the health and vitality of miniature roses. These plants require regular moisture to support their growth and flowering, but the amount and frequency of watering depend on various factors, including climate, soil type, and the specific needs of the roses. Understanding these factors and adjusting the watering schedule accordingly ensures that the roses receive the optimal amount of water throughout the growing season.

Watering is an essential part of routine care to maintain the freshness of roses

In general, miniature roses should be watered deeply and thoroughly, ensuring that the water reaches the root zone. This encourages deep root growth and helps the plants become more drought-tolerant. Watering deeply also reduces the frequency of watering, as the soil retains moisture for a longer period. The goal is to keep the soil consistently moist but not waterlogged, as excessive moisture can lead to root rot and other problems. Monitoring the soil moisture regularly and adjusting the watering schedule based on weather conditions is key to successful rose care.

The time of day for watering is also an important consideration. Watering early in the morning is generally recommended, as it allows the plants to absorb moisture before the heat of the day. Morning watering also gives the foliage time to dry out, reducing the risk of fungal diseases. Evening watering can be effective in hot climates, but care should be taken to avoid wet foliage overnight, as this can promote disease. Choosing the optimal time for watering helps in maximizing the benefits and minimizing potential issues.

Using the right watering techniques ensures that the water is delivered efficiently and effectively. Drip irrigation systems are highly recommended for miniature roses, as they provide a slow, steady supply of water directly to the root zone. This method reduces water wastage and minimizes the risk of wetting the foliage, which can lead to disease. Soaker hoses are another effective option, allowing water to seep slowly into the soil. Hand watering with a watering can or hose fitted with a fine rose can also be effective, provided the water is applied gently and evenly.

Mulching plays a crucial role in maintaining soil moisture and reducing the need for frequent watering. A layer of organic mulch, such as compost, straw, or wood chips, helps retain moisture in the soil, reduce evaporation, and keep the soil temperature stable. Mulch also suppresses weeds, which can compete with roses for water and nutrients. Maintaining a mulch layer of 2 to 3 inches thick around the base of the roses provides ongoing benefits throughout the growing season. Mulch is a simple yet effective practice that supports the health and well-being of the roses.

Adjusting the watering schedule based on the growth stage of the roses is also important. Newly planted roses require more frequent watering to establish their root systems, while established roses can be watered less often but more deeply. During periods of active growth and flowering, the water needs of the roses may increase. Conversely, during dormancy or cooler weather, the watering frequency can be reduced. Understanding the specific needs of the roses at different stages of their growth helps in providing the right amount of water.

Monitoring the plants and soil regularly for signs of overwatering or underwatering is essential. Wilting, yellowing leaves, or poor growth can indicate a problem with the watering schedule. Adjusting the amount and frequency of watering based on these observations ensures that the roses receive the optimal care. Regularly checking the soil moisture and responding to the needs of the plants helps in maintaining healthy, vibrant miniature roses. A well-managed watering schedule is a cornerstone of successful rose gardening.

Fertilizing Your Miniature Roses

Proper fertilization is key to promoting the growth and flowering of miniature roses. These plants require a balanced supply of nutrients to support their development and produce abundant blooms. Understanding the nutritional needs of miniature roses and providing the right type and amount of fertilizer ensures that they remain healthy and vigorous throughout the growing season. A well-planned fertilization schedule is essential for achieving the best results.

The three primary nutrients that roses require are nitrogen (N), phosphorus (P), and potassium (K). Nitrogen promotes healthy leaf and stem growth, phosphorus supports root development and flowering, and potassium enhances overall plant health and disease resistance. A balanced fertilizer that provides these nutrients in the right proportions is ideal for miniature roses. Fertilizers labeled as "rose food" are specifically formulated to meet the needs of roses and are a good choice for consistent feeding.

Organic fertilizers, such as compost, manure, and fish emulsion, offer a slow-release source of nutrients that benefit the soil as well as the plants. These fertilizers improve soil structure, enhance microbial activity, and provide a steady supply of nutrients over time. Incorporating organic matter into the soil before planting and using organic fertilizers throughout the growing season supports the long-term health of the roses. Organic fertilization practices are environmentally friendly and contribute to sustainable gardening.

The timing of fertilization is crucial for supporting the growth and flowering of miniature roses. Fertilizing in early spring, as new growth begins, provides a nutrient boost that encourages vigorous development. A second application in late spring to early summer supports the main flowering period. Additional feedings can be done every four to six weeks during the growing season, depending on the needs of the plants and the type of fertilizer used. Avoiding fertilization in late fall helps prevent new growth that could be damaged by frost.

Applying fertilizer correctly is important to avoid over-fertilization, which can harm the plants. Granular fertilizers should be spread evenly around the base of the rose, avoiding direct contact with the stems and leaves. Watering the fertilizer in thoroughly ensures that the nutrients are absorbed by the roots. Liquid fertilizers can be applied directly to the soil or as a foliar spray, but care should be taken to follow the manufacturer's instructions for dilution and application rates. Proper application techniques ensure that the roses receive the nutrients they need without risk of fertilizer burn.

Monitoring the roses for signs of nutrient deficiencies helps in adjusting the fertilization schedule. Yellowing leaves, poor growth, or reduced flowering can indicate a lack of essential nutrients. Soil testing can provide valuable information about nutrient levels and help in identifying any deficiencies. Based on the results, specific amendments can be made to address the nutrient needs of the roses. Regular observation and testing ensure that the fertilization program remains effective and responsive to the plants' requirements.

Combining fertilization with other good gardening practices enhances the overall health and performance of miniature roses. Adequate watering, proper soil preparation, and mulching all contribute to the effective uptake of nutrients. Healthy, well-maintained plants are better able to utilize the nutrients provided by fertilizers, resulting in robust growth and abundant blooms. Integrating fertilization into a comprehensive care routine maximizes the benefits and ensures that the roses thrive.

Using fertilizers responsibly is important for protecting the environment. Avoiding over-application and runoff into water sources helps prevent pollution and supports sustainable gardening practices. Organic fertilizers and environmentally friendly products are preferable choices that minimize the impact on the ecosystem.

Pruning and Deadheading for Continuous Blooms

Pruning is a vital practice for maintaining the health and vigor of miniature roses. Regular pruning encourages new growth, improves air circulation, and shapes the plant for optimal flowering. Understanding the principles of pruning and applying the right techniques ensures that the roses remain productive and attractive. Pruning helps in removing dead, damaged, or diseased wood, preventing the spread of disease and promoting healthy growth.

The best time to prune miniature roses is in early spring, just as new growth begins to emerge. This timing allows the gardener to assess the plant's structure and remove any winter damage. Using clean, sharp bypass pruners, make cuts at a 45-degree angle just above an outward-facing bud.

This encourages the new growth to develop outward, creating an open and airy structure. Removing any crossing or crowded branches improves air circulation and reduces the risk of disease.

Pruning is essential for preserving the health and vitality of miniature roses.

Deadheading, or removing spent blooms, is another important practice that promotes continuous flowering. Miniature roses are capable of producing multiple bloom cycles throughout the growing season if regularly deadheaded. Using scissors or pruners, cut the spent flower stem back to the first set of healthy leaves or a bud that faces outward. This encourages the plant to redirect its energy into producing new blooms rather than forming seed pods. Regular deadheading keeps the plant looking tidy and prolongs the flowering period.

Pruning also involves shaping the plant to maintain its desired form and size. For container-grown roses, keeping the plant compact and well-balanced is important for aesthetic reasons and to prevent overcrowding. For garden-planted roses, maintaining a shape that allows for good light penetration and air circulation is essential. Light pruning throughout the growing season can help maintain the desired shape and encourage bushy growth. Understanding the growth habits of the specific rose variety helps in applying the right pruning techniques.

Addressing any issues such as suckers, which are vigorous shoots that emerge from the rootstock below the graft union, is also part of regular pruning. Suckers can drain energy from the main plant and should be removed as soon as they are noticed. Gently pull or cut the suckers at their base to prevent them from regrowing. Keeping the area around the base of the rose clear of debris and weeds also helps in preventing the growth of suckers and other unwanted shoots.

Pruning for rejuvenation may be necessary for older or neglected roses. This involves more drastic pruning to remove old, woody stems and encourage new growth from the base. Cutting back the plant by about one-third to one-half can stimulate vigorous new growth and revitalized flowering. This type of pruning should be done in early spring before the plant begins active growth. Rejuvenation pruning can breathe new life into an older rose and restore its productivity and beauty.

Regular pruning and deadheading, combined with proper watering, fertilization, and pest management, create the conditions for continuous blooming and healthy growth. Observing the plants and responding to their needs ensures that they remain vibrant and productive throughout the growing season.

Chapter 5

Container Gardening with Miniature Roses

Choosing the Right Containers

Growing Beautiful Miniature Rose in Containers

Selecting the appropriate container for miniature roses is fundamental to their health and growth. Containers come in various materials, such as plastic, terracotta, ceramic, and wood, each offering distinct benefits. Plastic containers are lightweight, durable, and often more affordable, making them a practical choice for many gardeners. However, they may not provide the same aesthetic appeal or breathability as other materials. Terracotta and ceramic pots offer a classic look and better aeration for the roots but can be heavier and more prone to breakage. Wood containers provide natural insulation, helping to maintain consistent soil temperatures, but they require treatment to prevent rot and extend their lifespan.

The size of the container is also crucial for the successful growth of miniature roses. A container that is too small can restrict root development, leading to poor growth and reduced flowering. Conversely, a container that is too large may retain excess moisture, increasing the risk of root rot. Generally, a pot with a diameter of at least 12 inches and a similar depth is suitable for most miniature roses. This size provides ample space for root growth while ensuring the plant has enough soil to retain moisture and nutrients.

Drainage is another vital aspect to consider when choosing a container. Proper drainage prevents water from accumulating at the bottom of the pot, which can cause root rot and other issues. Containers should have multiple drainage holes to allow excess water to escape easily. Adding a layer of gravel or broken pottery at the bottom of the pot can further enhance drainage. Ensuring adequate drainage is essential for maintaining the health of potted miniature roses, preventing waterlogging, and promoting healthy root development.

The aesthetics of the container should not be overlooked, as it can enhance the visual appeal of the garden. The choice of container should complement the overall design and style of the garden or indoor space. Whether opting for a modern, sleek look with metal or plastic pots or a more traditional appearance with terracotta or wooden containers, the right choice can add to the beauty of the miniature roses. The container serves not only as a functional piece but also as an integral part of the garden's visual composition.

Portability is an important factor for those who need to move their plants frequently. Lightweight containers, such as those made from plastic or fiberglass, are easier to transport, making them ideal for balconies, patios, and indoor spaces where repositioning might be necessary. Heavier containers, like ceramic or terracotta, are more stable and less likely to tip over in windy conditions, making them suitable for permanent outdoor placements. Assessing the need for mobility helps in selecting the most practical container type.

Insulation properties of the container material can affect the plant's health, particularly in extreme weather conditions. Terracotta and wood provide good insulation, helping to keep roots cooler in summer and warmer in winter. Plastic pots, while durable, can heat up quickly in direct sunlight, potentially damaging the roots. Using double-walled plastic pots or placing them in shaded areas can mitigate this effect. Choosing containers with good insulating properties ensures that the roots are protected from temperature fluctuations.

Considering the container's durability is important for long-term gardening. High-quality materials that can withstand outdoor conditions, such as UV-resistant plastic or treated wood, will last longer and require less frequent replacement. Investing in durable containers reduces the need for frequent repotting and ensures that the miniature roses have a stable growing environment. Durability, combined with aesthetics and functionality, makes for a well-chosen container that supports the healthy growth of miniature roses.

Soil Mixes for Potted Miniature Roses

Creating the right soil mix is essential for the successful growth of potted miniature roses. A well-balanced soil mix provides the necessary nutrients, aeration, and moisture retention that these plants need. A typical mix for miniature roses includes garden loam, peat moss, and perlite or vermiculite in equal parts. This combination ensures good drainage while retaining sufficient moisture and providing a stable structure for root growth. The loam offers essential nutrients, peat moss improves moisture retention, and perlite or vermiculite enhances aeration and drainage.

Organic matter is a crucial component of any soil mix for miniature roses. Adding compost or well-rotted manure to the mix can significantly enhance its fertility and structure. Organic matter provides a slow-release source of nutrients and supports beneficial microbial activity in the soil. This helps in creating a healthy and balanced growing environment for the roses. Incorporating organic amendments into the soil mix ensures that the plants receive a steady supply of nutrients over time, promoting robust growth and flowering.

The pH level of the soil mix is another important factor to consider. Miniature roses prefer a slightly acidic to neutral pH range, typically between 6.0 and 6.5. Testing the soil mix and adjusting the pH as needed can optimize the growing conditions for the roses. If the pH is too high (alkaline), adding sulfur or peat moss can help lower it. Conversely, if the pH is too low (acidic), incorporating lime can raise it. Maintaining the appropriate pH level ensures that the roses can absorb nutrients effectively.

Drainage is critical in a soil mix for container gardening, as poor drainage can lead to waterlogged roots and root rot. Incorporating coarse sand or fine gravel into the mix can enhance its drainage properties. Ensuring that the soil remains loose and well-aerated allows excess water to drain away, preventing waterlogging while retaining enough moisture for the plant's needs. Regularly checking the soil moisture and adjusting the watering schedule accordingly helps maintain optimal moisture levels.

Fertilizing potted miniature roses is essential due to the limited nutrient availability in containers. A balanced, slow-release fertilizer incorporated into the soil mix provides a steady supply of nutrients. Additionally, liquid fertilizers can be applied during the growing season to support vigorous growth and flowering. Organic fertilizers, such as fish emulsion or seaweed extract, offer a gentle and sustainable nutrient source. Combining these with a well-prepared soil mix ensures that the roses receive all the necessary nutrients.

Soil mixes should be refreshed periodically to maintain their fertility and structure. Over time, the organic matter in the mix decomposes, and the soil can become compacted, reducing its effectiveness. Repotting the roses every couple of years, replacing the old soil with fresh mix, helps maintain a healthy growing environment. During repotting, it is also an opportunity to inspect the roots, prune any that are damaged or overgrown, and ensure the plant remains healthy and vigorous.

Customizing the soil mix to meet the specific needs of miniature roses enhances their overall health and performance. Experimenting with different proportions of ingredients and observing the plants' responses can help in fine-tuning the mix. Providing a well-balanced, nutrient-rich, and well-draining soil mix is fundamental to the success of container-grown miniature roses. The right soil mix supports healthy root development, robust growth, and abundant blooms.

Tips for Indoor and Balcony Gardening

Gardening with miniature roses indoors or on balconies requires specific considerations to ensure the plants thrive in these environments. Light is one of the most critical factors for successful indoor and balcony gardening. Miniature roses need at least six hours of direct sunlight each day. Placing the plants near south-facing windows or on sunny balconies maximizes their exposure to natural light. If natural light is insufficient, using grow lights can provide the necessary illumination. Full-spectrum LED grow lights are an excellent option, as they mimic natural sunlight and support healthy growth.

Temperature control is another important aspect of indoor and balcony gardening. Miniature roses prefer temperatures between 65°F and 75°F during the day and slightly cooler temperatures at night. Avoid placing the plants near drafty windows, heating vents, or air conditioners, as sudden temperature fluctuations can stress the plants. On balconies, providing shade during the hottest part of the day can prevent heat stress, while bringing the plants indoors during extreme cold protects them from frost.

Maintaining a stable temperature range supports the overall health of the roses.

Humidity levels can also impact the growth of indoor and balcony roses. Indoor environments, especially those with central heating or air conditioning, can have low humidity levels that may cause the plants to dry out. Using a humidity tray filled with water or a room humidifier can help maintain adequate humidity around the plants. On balconies, misting the roses in the early morning can provide additional moisture without causing prolonged wetness. Proper humidity management helps prevent issues such as dry leaf edges and encourages healthy growth.

Watering indoor and balcony roses requires careful attention to avoid overwatering or underwatering. The restricted root space in containers means that the soil can dry out more quickly, but overwatering can lead to root rot. Monitoring the soil moisture regularly and adjusting the watering schedule based on the conditions is essential. Watering thoroughly until water drains out of the bottom ensures that the entire root zone is moistened. Allowing the top inch of soil to dry out between waterings helps prevent waterlogging and maintains a healthy balance.

Fertilizing container-grown roses is important due to the limited nutrient availability in pots. Regular feeding with a balanced, water-soluble fertilizer supports continuous growth and flowering. Organic fertilizers, such as fish emulsion or liquid seaweed, provide a gentle nutrient boost and improve soil health. Fertilizing every four to six weeks during the growing season helps maintain nutrient levels and promotes vigorous growth.

Ensuring that the roses receive consistent nutrition supports their health and enhances their blooming potential.

Pest management is crucial for indoor and balcony gardening, where plants can be more vulnerable to pests due to the confined space. Regularly inspecting the roses for signs of pests, such as aphids, spider mites, and whiteflies, helps in early detection and control. Using organic pest control methods, such as neem oil or insecticidal soap, can effectively manage infestations without harming the environment. Maintaining good air circulation and keeping the plants clean also reduces the risk of pest problems.

Maximizing the visual appeal of indoor and balcony gardens involves thoughtful arrangement and design. Grouping miniature roses with other compatible plants creates a lush, vibrant display. Using decorative containers and incorporating elements such as trellises or hanging baskets can add vertical interest and optimize space. Considering the overall aesthetic and functionality of the space ensures that the garden is both beautiful and practical.

Chapter 6

Dealing with Pests and Diseases

Common Pests and How to Identify Them

Miniature roses, like all plants, are susceptible to various pests that can damage their health and appearance. One of the most common pests is the aphid, a small, soft-bodied insect that feeds on plant sap. Aphids can be green, black, brown, or red and are often found in clusters on new growth, flower buds, and the undersides of leaves. Their feeding can cause distorted growth, yellowing leaves, and reduced vigor. Aphids also excrete a sticky substance called honeydew, which can attract ants and lead to the growth of sooty mold.

Spider mites are another common pest that can affect miniature roses. These tiny arachnids are difficult to see with the naked eye but can cause significant damage. They feed on plant sap, causing stippling and yellowing of the leaves, which may eventually lead to leaf drop. Spider mites thrive in hot, dry conditions, and their presence is often indicated by fine webbing on the undersides of leaves. Early detection and control are essential to prevent severe infestations.

Thrips are small, slender insects that feed on flowers and foliage, causing discoloration and deformation. They are particularly troublesome for roses, as they can damage flower buds and petals, leading to poor-quality blooms. Thrips are usually yellow, brown, or black and are difficult to detect due to their size and rapid movement. They often hide within flower buds, making them challenging to control. Identifying thrips early and implementing appropriate measures can help protect the roses from damage.

Rose slugs, which are the larvae of sawflies, can cause significant defoliation of miniature roses. These small, greenish caterpillars feed on the underside of leaves, creating a skeletonized appearance. Severe infestations can lead to extensive leaf loss and weakened plants. Rose slugs are most active in spring and early summer, and their presence can be identified by the damage they cause. Handpicking and targeted insecticidal treatments can effectively manage rose slug populations.

Japanese beetles are a well-known pest of roses, feeding on both the foliage and flowers. These metallic green and copper-colored beetles are easily recognizable and can cause extensive damage in a short period. They chew on leaves, creating a lace-like appearance, and can also damage flower petals. Japanese beetles are most active during the summer months and can be controlled through handpicking, traps, and insecticidal treatments. Monitoring and managing their populations help protect the roses from significant damage.

Caterpillars, including various species of moth and butterfly larvae, can also be problematic for miniature roses. These pests feed on the leaves, stems, and flowers, causing noticeable damage. While some caterpillars are easy to spot due to their size and color, others may be more camouflaged. Identifying the specific type of caterpillar and implementing appropriate control measures, such as biological controls or targeted insecticides, can help manage their populations. Regular inspections and prompt action can prevent caterpillar infestations from becoming severe.

Effective pest management for miniature roses involves a combination of monitoring, identification, and control strategies. Regularly inspecting the plants for signs of pests and taking prompt action can prevent minor infestations from escalating. Using organic and environmentally friendly control methods, such as insecticidal soaps, neem oil, and beneficial insects, helps protect the roses while minimizing harm to the ecosystem. Maintaining healthy, well-cared-for plants can also reduce their susceptibility to pests, supporting robust growth and flowering.

Disease Prevention and Treatment

Preventing and treating diseases in miniature roses is crucial for maintaining their health and ensuring continuous blooms. One of the most common diseases affecting roses is black spot, caused by the fungus Diplocarpon rosae. Black spot manifests as dark, circular spots with fringed edges on the leaves, leading to yellowing and premature leaf drop. The disease thrives in humid, wet conditions, making prevention through proper cultural practices essential. Ensuring good air circulation around the plants, avoiding overhead watering, and removing infected leaves can help manage black spot.

Powdery mildew is another prevalent disease that affects roses, characterized by a white, powdery coating on the leaves, stems, and buds. This fungal disease can distort growth and reduce the plant's vigor. Powdery mildew thrives in warm, dry conditions, often appearing in late spring and early summer. Preventive measures include ensuring adequate spacing between plants, providing good air circulation, and applying preventive fungicides if necessary. Regular monitoring and early treatment can prevent the disease from spreading.

Rust is a fungal disease that causes orange or rust-colored pustules on the undersides of leaves. It can lead to leaf drop and weakened plants if not controlled. Rust thrives in moist, cool conditions, often appearing in spring and fall. Managing rust involves removing and destroying infected leaves, improving air circulation, and applying fungicides as needed. Regular inspection and prompt action can keep rust under control, protecting the health of the roses.

Botrytis blight, also known as gray mold, affects roses during cool, damp weather. It causes grayish-brown spots on flowers, buds, and leaves, leading to rotting and decay. Botrytis blight can be particularly damaging to flower buds, preventing them from opening. Preventive measures include ensuring good air circulation, avoiding overhead watering, and removing and destroying infected plant material. Applying fungicides can help manage severe infections, but cultural practices are the first line of defense.

Canker diseases, caused by various fungi, affect the stems and can cause dieback and plant death. Cankers appear as sunken, discolored areas on the stems, often with a rough or cracked texture. They can girdle the stem, cutting off the flow of water and nutrients. Pruning out infected stems and ensuring good plant health through proper watering, fertilization, and pest management can help prevent cankers. Avoiding mechanical injuries to the stems and applying protective fungicides can also reduce the risk of infection.

Verticillium wilt is a soil-borne fungal disease that causes wilting and yellowing of the leaves, often leading to plant death. It infects the plant through the roots and disrupts water uptake. There is no cure for verticillium wilt, so prevention is crucial. Choosing disease-resistant varieties, avoiding planting roses in areas where the disease has been present, and maintaining good soil health can help prevent infection. Removing and destroying infected plants and improving soil drainage can also reduce the risk.

Implementing integrated disease management strategies is essential for maintaining healthy miniature roses. This includes selecting disease-resistant varieties, practicing good sanitation, providing optimal growing conditions, and using fungicides when necessary. Regular monitoring and early intervention are key to preventing the spread of diseases. Maintaining healthy plants through proper watering, fertilization, and pest management enhances their natural defenses against diseases, ensuring robust growth and abundant blooms.

Organic vs. Chemical Solutions

Managing pests and diseases in miniature roses involves choosing between organic and chemical solutions, each with its advantages and considerations. Organic solutions are derived from natural sources and aim to manage pests and diseases with minimal environmental impact. These include insecticidal soaps, neem oil, horticultural oils, and biological controls such as beneficial insects. Organic solutions are generally safer for humans, pets, and beneficial wildlife, making them a preferred choice for environmentally conscious gardeners.

Insecticidal soaps and horticultural oils are effective against a wide range of pests, including aphids, spider mites, and whiteflies. These products work by disrupting the pests' cell membranes or smothering them. They are biodegradable and break down quickly, reducing the risk of environmental contamination. Neem oil, derived from the neem tree, has insecticidal, fungicidal, and miticidal properties, making it a versatile option for managing various pests and diseases. Regular applications can help keep pest populations under control while minimizing harm to beneficial insects.

Biological controls involve the use of natural predators, parasites, or pathogens to manage pest populations. Ladybugs, lacewings, and predatory mites are examples of beneficial insects that feed on common rose pests. Introducing these beneficial organisms into the garden can provide long-term pest control without the need for chemical interventions. Encouraging biodiversity and creating a habitat that supports beneficial insects can enhance the effectiveness of biological controls. This approach promotes a balanced ecosystem and reduces the reliance on chemical treatments.

Organic fungicides, such as copper-based sprays and sulfur, are effective against fungal diseases like black spot, powdery mildew, and rust. These products are less harmful to the environment than synthetic fungicides and can be used as part of an integrated disease management strategy. Regular applications, combined with cultural practices like proper spacing, good air circulation, and sanitation, can help prevent and manage fungal infections. Organic fungicides provide a sustainable option for disease control while maintaining soil and plant health.

Chemical solutions, including synthetic insecticides and fungicides, offer quick and effective control of pests and diseases. These products are formulated to target specific pests or pathogens and can provide rapid relief from severe infestations. However, chemical solutions can have broader environmental impacts, including the potential to harm beneficial insects, pollinators, and other non-target organisms. Careful selection and application of chemical treatments are essential to minimize these risks. Following label instructions and applying chemicals only when necessary can help reduce negative environmental effects.

Systemic insecticides and fungicides are chemical solutions that are absorbed by the plant and provide long-lasting protection. These products can be particularly effective against pests and diseases that are difficult to control with surface treatments. However, systemic chemicals can persist in the environment and potentially affect non-target organisms. Using systemic products judiciously and in combination with other control methods can help manage pests and diseases while reducing reliance on chemicals.

Integrated Pest Management (IPM) combines organic and chemical solutions to achieve effective and sustainable pest and disease control. This approach emphasizes prevention, monitoring, and targeted treatments, using chemical solutions as a last resort. IPM promotes the use of cultural practices, biological controls, and organic treatments to manage pests and diseases while minimizing environmental impact. Implementing IPM strategies helps maintain healthy miniature roses, protect beneficial organisms, and create a balanced garden ecosystem.

Chapter 7

Advanced Growing Techniques

Propagating Miniature Roses

Propagation of Miniature Roses with Stem Cuttings

Propagating miniature roses can be an immensely rewarding practice, allowing gardeners to expand their collections and share beloved varieties with others. One of the most common methods of propagation is through stem cuttings. This technique involves selecting healthy, non-flowering shoots, usually about six inches long, and cutting them just below a leaf node. The leaves from the lower part of the cutting are removed to expose the nodes, which is where root formation will occur. The cuttings are then dipped in rooting hormone to enhance root development and planted in a well-draining medium, such as a mix of perlite and peat moss.

Ensuring the right environment for the cuttings is crucial for successful propagation. The planted cuttings should be kept in a warm, humid environment, away from direct sunlight. Covering them with a plastic dome or placing them in a greenhouse can help maintain the necessary humidity levels. Consistent moisture is essential, so the medium should be kept slightly moist but not waterlogged. Within a few weeks, roots should begin to form, and new growth will be visible, indicating successful propagation.

Another effective method for propagating miniature roses is through layering. This involves bending a low-growing shoot to the ground and burying a portion of it while it is still attached to the parent plant. The buried section of the stem should have a few leaves removed and may be lightly wounded to encourage rooting. The buried section is then secured with a pin or stone and covered with soil. Over time, roots will develop from the buried nodes, and once the new plant is well-established, it can be severed from the parent plant and transplanted.

Propagating through seeds is less common due to the genetic variability and longer time required for seedlings to mature. However, it can be an exciting way to develop new rose varieties. Seeds are harvested from hips, cleaned, and stratified by chilling them in a refrigerator for several weeks to simulate winter conditions. After stratification, the seeds are sown in a sterile seed-starting mix and kept in a warm, well-lit area. Germination can take several weeks, and the resulting seedlings may exhibit diverse characteristics, offering a unique propagation experience.

Micropropagation, or tissue culture, is an advanced technique used primarily by commercial growers. This method involves taking small tissue samples from a parent plant and placing them in a sterile, nutrient-rich medium under controlled conditions. The tissue fragments develop into small plantlets, which are then transferred to soil to grow into mature plants. Micropropagation allows for the rapid production of large numbers of identical plants, making it a valuable tool for preserving rare varieties and mass production.

Maintaining genetic integrity is an important consideration in propagation. Cuttings and layering produce clones of the parent plant, ensuring that the new plants retain the desired characteristics. Seed propagation, on the other hand, introduces genetic variation, which can be both a challenge and an opportunity for developing new traits. Understanding the goals of propagation—whether to reproduce specific characteristics or experiment with new varieties—helps in selecting the appropriate method.

Propagating miniature roses is not only a practical way to expand a garden but also a deeply satisfying activity. Each successful propagation is a testament to the gardener's skill and patience, offering the joy of nurturing new life from existing plants. This practice also fosters a deeper connection to the plants, as gardeners become intimately involved in their growth and development. The ability to propagate roses opens up endless possibilities for creativity and exploration in the garden.

Grafting and Budding Techniques

Grafting and budding are advanced horticultural techniques used to propagate roses and enhance their growth and blooming characteristics. Grafting involves joining two plant parts—the rootstock and the scion—so that they grow as a single plant. This method combines the desirable traits of both plants, such as disease resistance from the rootstock and superior blooms from the scion. The process begins with selecting healthy, compatible rootstock and scion. The scion, typically a stem from the desired rose variety, is cut to match the rootstock's incision. The two parts are then fitted together and secured with grafting tape to ensure they remain in contact as they heal and unite.

The grafting process requires precision and care to ensure successful fusion. The cambium layers of both the rootstock and scion must align perfectly, as this is where the growth tissues merge. Once grafted, the plant is placed in a controlled environment to heal. Maintaining optimal humidity and temperature levels is crucial during this period to prevent desiccation and encourage successful grafting. After a few weeks, the graft should be fully integrated, and the plant will begin to grow as a unified organism.

Budding, a specific type of grafting, involves inserting a single bud from the desired rose variety into a slit or notch made in the rootstock. This method is often used because it can be more efficient and requires less scion material than traditional grafting. The bud is carefully inserted into the incision and wrapped securely with grafting tape. As with grafting, the union must be kept moist and protected until the bud starts to grow.

Budding is typically done in late summer when the rootstock is actively growing, providing the best conditions for the bud to take hold.

Both grafting and budding offer several advantages for rose cultivation. These techniques can enhance plant vigor and productivity, as the rootstock can provide superior support and nutrient uptake. They also enable the propagation of roses that may not root well from cuttings or other methods. Additionally, grafting and budding can extend the lifespan of a rose variety by renewing it on a new root system, preserving its genetic material and desirable traits.

Choosing the right rootstock is crucial for successful grafting and budding. The rootstock should be compatible with the scion or bud and possess characteristics that improve the overall performance of the grafted plant. Commonly used rootstocks include Rosa multiflora and Rosa canina, known for their disease resistance, hardiness, and vigorous growth. The selection of rootstock can influence the growth rate, size, and adaptability of the grafted rose, making it an important factor in the success of these techniques.

Grafting and budding also require proper aftercare to ensure the new plant thrives. This includes monitoring for signs of stress or failure, such as wilting or discoloration, and providing appropriate support as the plant grows. Pruning may be necessary to remove any shoots that emerge from the rootstock, ensuring that all growth is directed to the scion or bud. Fertilization and watering should be adjusted to support the needs of the newly grafted plant, promoting robust growth and flowering.

These techniques represent a fusion of art and science, requiring skill, knowledge, and patience. The successful practice of grafting and budding can result in healthier, more vigorous plants with enhanced ornamental qualities. For gardeners and horticulturists, mastering these techniques offers the ability to innovate and improve their rose collections, contributing to the rich tradition of rose cultivation. The satisfaction of seeing a grafted or budded rose flourish is a rewarding experience, showcasing the potential of advanced horticultural practices.

Creating Bonsai Roses

Creating bonsai roses involves transforming miniature rose plants into stunning, miniature landscapes through careful training and pruning. This practice merges the art of bonsai with the beauty of roses, resulting in unique and captivating specimens. The process begins with selecting the right rose variety, typically a naturally compact and slow-growing miniature rose. These characteristics make it easier to train and maintain the plant's small size and intricate shape.

The initial step in creating a bonsai rose is to establish a strong root system. This is achieved by planting the rose in a small, shallow bonsai pot that restricts root growth, encouraging the development of fine feeder roots. The soil mix should be well-draining, typically composed of akadama, pumice, and lava rock, which provide aeration and moisture retention. Regular root pruning is essential to maintain the plant's compact size and health. This involves gently trimming the roots to prevent them from becoming pot-bound and promoting a balanced root system.

Pruning and shaping the foliage and stems are critical to achieving the desired bonsai form. This involves careful, precise cuts to control the growth direction and density of the branches. Techniques such as wiring can be used to guide the stems into artistic shapes, creating the illusion of age and natural beauty. The key is to balance the plant's natural growth tendencies with the desired aesthetic, ensuring that the overall form remains harmonious and proportional.

Beautiful Bonsai Rose

Maintaining a bonsai rose requires diligent care and attention to detail. Regular watering is crucial, as the small pot and well-draining soil can dry out quickly. Monitoring soil moisture and adjusting the watering schedule based on environmental conditions help keep the plant hydrated. Fertilization should be done sparingly, using a balanced, slow-release fertilizer to provide essential nutrients without encouraging excessive growth. Maintaining a consistent care routine supports the health and vigor of the bonsai rose.

Seasonal maintenance is also important in bonsai rose care. In spring, pruning and wiring are performed to shape the plant and promote new growth. During the growing season, regular pinching and trimming help maintain the desired form and prevent the plant from becoming overgrown. In autumn, a thorough pruning may be necessary to prepare the plant for winter dormancy. Protecting the bonsai rose from extreme temperatures and harsh conditions during winter ensures its survival and continued growth.

Creating a bonsai rose is not only a horticultural challenge but also an artistic endeavor. The process requires a deep understanding of the plant's growth habits and a creative vision for its final form. Each bonsai rose is a unique expression of the gardener's skill and aesthetic sensibility, reflecting the delicate balance between nature and art. The satisfaction of cultivating a beautifully crafted bonsai rose is a testament to the gardener's dedication and expertise.

The art of bonsai roses brings together the best of both worlds— the timeless elegance of bonsai and the vibrant beauty of roses. This fusion creates living sculptures that captivate and inspire, offering a unique way to enjoy and appreciate miniature roses. For gardeners and bonsai enthusiasts, the practice of creating bonsai roses represents a rewarding journey of learning, creativity, and connection with nature.

Chapter 8

Seasonal Care Routines

Spring: Preparing for Growth

Spring is a critical time for preparing miniature roses for the growing season, as it sets the foundation for robust growth and abundant blooms. As temperatures rise and daylight hours increase, roses emerge from their winter dormancy and begin to show signs of new growth. One of the first tasks in spring is to perform a thorough cleanup around the rose plants. This involves removing any winter mulch, dead leaves, and debris that may harbor pests and diseases. Cleaning up the garden bed helps improve air circulation and reduces the risk of fungal infections.

Pruning is a vital spring task that promotes healthy growth and flowering. It involves removing dead, damaged, or diseased wood and shaping the plant to encourage a well-balanced structure. Pruning cuts should be made just above an outward-facing bud, encouraging new growth to develop outward rather than inward. This practice helps maintain an open center, improving light penetration and air circulation within the plant. Pruning also stimulates the production of new canes, which are more vigorous and produce better blooms.

Fertilization is essential in spring to provide the nutrients that roses need for growth and flowering. Applying a balanced, slow-release fertilizer around the base of the plants ensures a steady supply of nutrients throughout the growing season. Organic fertilizers, such as compost or well-rotted manure, can be added to enrich the soil and improve its structure. Regular feeding during the active growing period supports robust growth and enhances bloom quality. Monitoring the plants for signs of nutrient deficiencies and adjusting the fertilization schedule as needed helps maintain their health.

Spring is also the time to inspect for pests and diseases that may have overwintered on the plants or in the soil. Common rose pests such as aphids, spider mites, and thrips can become active as temperatures rise. Regularly inspecting the plants and taking prompt action to manage any infestations is crucial. Using organic pest control methods, such as insecticidal soaps or neem oil, can effectively manage pests while minimizing harm to beneficial insects. Preventive measures, such as proper spacing and good air circulation, help reduce the risk of disease.

Mulching is an important spring task that helps conserve soil moisture, suppress weeds, and regulate soil temperature. Applying a layer of organic mulch, such as wood chips, straw, or compost, around the base of the roses provides these benefits while gradually enriching the soil as it decomposes. Mulch also protects the roots from temperature fluctuations and helps maintain a stable growing environment. Maintaining a mulch layer of 2 to 3 inches thick ensures optimal conditions for the roses.

Watering practices should be adjusted in spring to support the increasing water needs of the growing plants. Ensuring consistent moisture levels is crucial, as fluctuations can stress the plants and reduce bloom production. Deep, thorough watering encourages deep root growth and helps the plants become more drought-tolerant. Monitoring soil moisture and adjusting the watering schedule based on weather conditions and plant needs ensures that the roses receive adequate hydration without becoming waterlogged.

Overall plant care in spring includes monitoring for any signs of stress or nutrient deficiencies and responding promptly. Addressing issues early in the season helps prevent more significant problems later. Providing support for climbing or tall-growing varieties, such as trellises or stakes, ensures that the plants remain upright and well-supported. Establishing a comprehensive care routine in spring sets the stage for a successful growing season, leading to healthy, vibrant miniature roses.

Summer: Maintaining Health and Vigour

Summer is a time of active growth and blooming for miniature roses, requiring diligent care to maintain their health and vigor. As temperatures rise, ensuring adequate hydration is crucial. Roses need consistent moisture to support their growth and flowering, especially during hot, dry spells. Deep watering, preferably in the morning, helps the plants cope with the heat and reduces the risk of fungal diseases. Using drip irrigation or soaker hoses can deliver water directly to the root zone, minimizing evaporation and keeping the foliage dry.

Mulching continues to play a vital role in summer care. A thick layer of organic mulch helps retain soil moisture, suppress weeds, and regulate soil temperature. This is particularly important during the peak of summer when evaporation rates are high. Mulch also prevents soil compaction and improves soil structure over time. Regularly checking and replenishing the mulch layer ensures that it remains effective throughout the season, providing ongoing benefits to the roses.

Mulching miniature roses is essential for proper summer care

Feeding the roses with a balanced fertilizer is essential to support their vigorous growth and continuous blooming. A slow-release granular fertilizer can be applied at the beginning of summer to provide a steady supply of nutrients. Additionally, liquid fertilizers or foliar feeds can be used to give the plants a quick nutrient boost. Ensuring that the roses receive adequate nutrition helps them produce abundant, high-quality blooms. Monitoring for signs of nutrient deficiencies, such as yellowing leaves or poor growth, and adjusting the feeding regimen accordingly supports their health.

Pruning and deadheading are important tasks during the summer months. Regularly removing spent blooms encourages the plants to produce new flowers and prevents the formation of seed pods, which can drain the plant's energy. Light pruning can also help maintain the plant's shape and remove any dead or diseased wood. Ensuring that the plants are well-pruned improves air circulation and reduces the risk of disease, contributing to the overall health of the roses.

Pest and disease management requires vigilance in summer, as warm temperatures and humidity can encourage the proliferation of common rose pests and fungal infections. Regularly inspecting the plants for signs of aphids, spider mites, thrips, and other pests allows for early intervention. Using organic pest control methods, such as neem oil, insecticidal soap, or introducing beneficial insects, can help manage pest populations. Preventive fungicide applications may be necessary in humid climates to protect against black spot, powdery mildew, and rust.

Providing support for climbing and tall-growing roses is essential to prevent damage from strong winds or heavy blooms. Securing the canes to trellises or stakes with soft ties helps keep the plants upright and reduces the risk of breakage. Regularly checking and adjusting the ties ensures that they do not constrict the growth of the canes. Proper support not only protects the plants but also enhances their appearance, creating a neat and orderly garden.

Adjusting the care routine based on weather conditions is important for maintaining the health of the roses. During periods of extreme heat, providing temporary shade or using shade cloth can help protect the plants from sunburn and heat stress. Conversely, ensuring good drainage and protecting the plants from excessive rain can prevent waterlogging and root rot. Adapting the care routine to meet the changing needs of the plants throughout the summer helps ensure their continuous health and vigor.

Autumn: Preparing for Dormancy

Autumn is a transitional period for miniature roses, as they prepare for dormancy in the upcoming winter months. One of the first tasks in autumn is to reduce the frequency of fertilization. Applying a final dose of balanced fertilizer early in the season supports the last flush of blooms, but feeding should be tapered off as the season progresses. Reducing fertilization helps the plants prepare for dormancy, allowing them to harden off and conserve energy for the winter.

Pruning in autumn focuses on removing any dead, damaged, or diseased wood, as well as shaping the plant for the winter. However, heavy pruning should be avoided, as this can stimulate new growth that may not harden off before frost. Light pruning helps improve air circulation and reduces the risk of disease, while maintaining the overall structure of the plant. Removing any remaining spent blooms and seed pods also helps direct the plant's energy towards root and cane development.

Watering practices should be adjusted in autumn to support the transition to dormancy. While it is important to ensure the plants remain hydrated, especially during dry spells, reducing the frequency of watering helps signal the plants to slow down their growth. Deep watering less frequently encourages the roots to grow deeper, enhancing the plant's resilience to winter conditions. Monitoring soil moisture and adjusting the watering schedule based on weather conditions ensures that the plants receive adequate hydration without encouraging excessive growth.

Mulching in autumn provides insulation for the roots, protecting them from temperature fluctuations and extreme cold. Applying a thick layer of organic mulch around the base of the plants helps maintain stable soil temperatures and conserves moisture. Mulch also prevents soil erosion and suppresses weeds, contributing to the overall health of the roses. Ensuring that the mulch layer is well-maintained and replenishing it as needed prepares the plants for the winter ahead.

Protecting the roses from early frosts is crucial in autumn, particularly for varieties that are less cold-hardy. Covering the plants with frost cloths or burlap can provide additional protection during sudden cold snaps. Ensuring that the root zone is well-mulched and considering additional insulation, such as wrapping the base of the plants, can help protect against severe frost damage. Taking preventive measures helps safeguard the plants' health and prepares them for a successful dormancy period.

Inspecting the plants for pests and diseases before winter is important for preventing issues from carrying over into the next growing season. Removing any infected plant material and applying appropriate treatments can help manage pest and disease problems. Cleaning up the garden bed, including removing fallen leaves and debris, reduces the habitat for pests and pathogens. Maintaining good garden hygiene supports the health of the roses and prepares them for dormancy.

Adjusting the overall care routine to support the plants' transition to dormancy involves a combination of reduced watering, fertilization, and pruning, as well as enhanced protection and hygiene measures. Ensuring that the roses enter dormancy in a healthy state sets the foundation for robust growth and blooming in the spring. Providing the necessary care and protection during autumn helps the plants conserve energy and withstand the challenges of winter.

Winter: Protecting Your Roses

Winter protection is essential for ensuring the survival and health of miniature roses through the cold months. One of the primary tasks in winter is to protect the root zone from freezing temperatures. Applying a thick layer of mulch, such as straw, leaves, or wood chips, around the base of the plants provides insulation and helps maintain stable soil temperatures. In regions with severe winters, additional protective measures, such as covering the plants with burlap or frost cloth, may be necessary to shield them from extreme cold and wind.

For container-grown roses, providing winter protection involves moving the pots to a sheltered location, such as a garage, shed, or unheated greenhouse. If indoor space is not available, clustering the pots together and insulating them with materials such as bubble wrap or blankets can help protect the roots from freezing. Elevating the pots off the ground and placing them on insulating materials, such as foam or wooden boards, can also prevent cold damage. Ensuring adequate protection for container-grown roses helps them survive the winter and resume growth in the spring.

Pruning in winter should be minimal, focusing on removing any remaining dead or diseased wood. Major pruning is typically done in late winter or early spring when the risk of severe frost has passed. Light pruning in winter helps reduce the risk of disease and improves air circulation while avoiding stimulating new growth. Ensuring that the plants are well-shaped and free of damaged wood supports their health during dormancy.

Winter watering practices should be adjusted to reflect the reduced water needs of dormant plants. While it is important to prevent the soil from drying out completely, overwatering can lead to root rot and other issues. Watering should be done sparingly, ensuring that the soil remains slightly moist without becoming waterlogged. Monitoring soil moisture and adjusting the watering schedule based on weather conditions helps maintain the right balance, supporting the health of the dormant plants.

Winter is also a time to monitor for pests that may seek shelter in the garden. Inspecting the plants and garden area for signs of pests, such as rodents or overwintering insects, and taking appropriate measures to manage them can prevent damage. Using physical barriers, such as wire mesh or traps, can help protect the plants from pest activity. Maintaining good garden hygiene and cleanliness reduces the risk of pest problems during the winter months.

Providing support and protection for the plants during winter storms and heavy snowfall is important for preventing physical damage. Ensuring that the plants are well-staked and using protective covers can help shield them from strong winds and heavy snow. Regularly checking and adjusting the protective measures as needed helps maintain their effectiveness throughout the winter. Preventing physical damage from weather conditions supports the overall health of the roses.

Winter care involves a combination of protective measures, monitoring, and minimal maintenance to ensure that miniature roses remain healthy and resilient through the cold months. Preparing the plants adequately for winter dormancy and providing the necessary protection helps them conserve energy and withstand the challenges of winter. Ensuring that the roses are well-cared-for during winter sets the stage for vigorous growth and abundant blooms in the coming spring.

Chapter 9

Designing with Miniature Roses

Creating Stunning Rose Displays

Beautiful rose arrangements with miniature roses.

Creating visually stunning rose displays with miniature roses involves thoughtful planning and artistic arrangement. The compact size and diverse color palette of miniature roses make them ideal for creating vibrant and intricate displays that can enhance any garden space. When designing a rose display, consider the overall theme and style of your garden. For formal gardens, symmetrical arrangements with evenly spaced plants can create a structured and elegant look. In contrast, informal or cottage-style gardens benefit from more relaxed, flowing arrangements that blend miniature roses with other complementary plants.

Color selection is a crucial element in creating captivating rose displays. Miniature roses are available in a wide range of colors, from classic reds and pinks to vibrant yellows, oranges, and whites. Combining different colors can create striking visual contrasts or harmonious blends, depending on the desired effect. For a bold display, use complementary colors like purple and yellow or red and green. For a more soothing and cohesive look, choose analogous colors that are next to each other on the color wheel, such as pink, red, and orange.

The height and form of the miniature roses should also be considered when planning a display. Grouping roses of varying heights can add depth and dimension to the arrangement. Taller varieties can be placed at the back or center of a display, with shorter ones around the edges to create a layered effect. Mixing different forms, such as single blooms and cluster-flowering varieties, can add textural interest and variety. Paying attention to the growth habits and bloom characteristics of each variety ensures a balanced and visually appealing display.

Seasonality plays a significant role in designing rose displays. Planning for continuous bloom throughout the growing season involves selecting varieties with staggered blooming times. Early, mid, and late-season bloomers can be combined to ensure that there is always something in flower. Additionally, incorporating roses with different blooming cycles, such as repeat bloomers and once-blooming varieties, can provide a dynamic and ever-changing display. This approach not only enhances the visual appeal but also extends the enjoyment of the garden.

Containers and hanging baskets offer versatile options for creating rose displays in small spaces or urban environments. Miniature roses are well-suited for container gardening, allowing for flexibility in placement and design. Decorative pots, urns, and hanging baskets can be used to create focal points on patios, balconies, or garden paths. Arranging multiple containers of varying sizes and heights can create a cohesive and layered look. The portability of containers allows for easy re-arrangement and adaptation to seasonal changes.

Incorporating complementary plants can enhance the beauty of rose displays. Companion plants, such as lavender, salvia, and catmint, can add color, texture, and fragrance, while also providing benefits like pest deterrence and improved soil health. Ground covers and low-growing perennials can fill in gaps and create a lush, cohesive appearance. Selecting plants that thrive in similar growing conditions ensures that all elements of the display flourish together. Thoughtful companion planting can elevate the overall aesthetic and health of the rose display.

Lighting can dramatically impact the presentation of rose displays, particularly in evening gardens. Installing landscape lighting, such as spotlights or string lights, can highlight the beauty of the roses and create a magical atmosphere. Lighting can accentuate the colors and forms of the roses, making the display enjoyable even after sunset. Strategic placement of lights ensures that key features of the display are illuminated, enhancing the overall visual impact. Considering the interplay of light and shadow adds an extra dimension to the design.

Integrating Miniature Roses in Mixed Borders

Integrating Miniature Roses in Mixed Borders

Integrating miniature roses into mixed borders involves combining them with a variety of plants to create a diverse and visually appealing garden landscape. Mixed borders are designed to include a range of plant types, such as perennials, annuals, shrubs, and bulbs, providing continuous interest throughout the growing season. Miniature roses can play a central role in these borders, offering vibrant color and structure while complementing the other plants in the arrangement.

When planning a mixed border, consider the overall color scheme and how the miniature roses will fit into it. The wide range of rose colors allows for creative combinations with other flowering plants. For instance, pairing pink or red roses with blue and purple perennials like delphiniums and salvia creates a striking contrast. Alternatively, using white or pastel-colored roses with silver foliage plants like artemisia or lamb's ear can create a soft and elegant look. Harmonizing the colors ensures a cohesive and visually pleasing design.

The height and growth habit of miniature roses should be considered to ensure a balanced and layered border. Place taller varieties at the back or middle of the border, with shorter plants in front to create a graduated effect. This layering provides depth and prevents taller plants from overshadowing shorter ones. Additionally, mixing upright roses with spreading or cascading varieties adds textural interest and prevents a monotonous appearance. Understanding the growth habits of each plant helps in creating a well-structured and dynamic border.

Companion planting is a key aspect of integrating roses into mixed borders. Choosing plants that have similar growing requirements ensures that all elements of the border thrive together. For example, miniature roses prefer well-draining soil and full sun, so companion plants should have similar needs. Perennials like echinacea, coreopsis, and daylilies are excellent choices, as they can provide continuous color and complement the roses. Incorporating plants with different foliage textures and shapes adds variety and enhances the overall aesthetic.

In addition to flowering plants, incorporating ornamental grasses and foliage plants can add movement and structure to mixed borders. Grasses like miscanthus or fountain grass provide a graceful backdrop and contrast to the rigid form of roses. Foliage plants with interesting colors or patterns, such as hostas or heucheras, can add depth and visual interest. These plants not only enhance the appearance of the border but also contribute to its ecological diversity, supporting beneficial insects and wildlife.

Seasonal planning ensures that the mixed border remains attractive throughout the year. Selecting plants with different blooming periods and foliage interest extends the display beyond the rose's blooming season. Spring bulbs like tulips and daffodils can provide early color, while autumn-flowering perennials like asters and sedums extend the interest into late fall. Including evergreen shrubs or winter-interest plants like hellebores ensures that the border has structure and beauty even in the off-season.

Maintaining a mixed border with roses involves regular care and attention to ensure all plants remain healthy and vibrant. This includes watering, mulching, and feeding according to the needs of the different plants. Pruning and deadheading roses and other flowering plants promote continuous blooming and neatness. Monitoring for pests and diseases is essential to prevent problems from spreading. Regular maintenance helps maintain the health and appearance of the border, allowing it to thrive and provide enjoyment year-round.

Using Miniature Roses in Floral Arrangements

Miniature roses are an excellent choice for creating beautiful and elegant floral arrangements due to their compact size and variety of colors. These roses can be used as the focal point in bouquets, centerpieces, and other floral designs, adding a touch of sophistication and charm. When creating floral arrangements, it is important to choose roses that are at the peak of their bloom, as this ensures the longest vase life and the most vibrant display.

To begin creating a floral arrangement with miniature roses, start by selecting a variety of flowers and foliage that complement the roses. Consider the color scheme and overall aesthetic you wish to achieve. For a classic look, pair red or white miniature roses with greenery like eucalyptus or ferns. For a more vibrant and eclectic arrangement, mix roses of different colors with bright, contrasting flowers like gerbera daisies, alstroemeria, or snapdragons. Adding different textures and forms enhances the visual interest and depth of the arrangement.

Preparing the roses and other flowers is crucial for the longevity of the arrangement. Trim the stems of the roses at an angle to increase the surface area for water absorption and remove any leaves that will be below the waterline to prevent bacterial growth. Conditioning the flowers by placing them in clean, lukewarm water with floral preservative for a few hours helps them hydrate fully before arranging. Ensuring the flowers are well-prepared helps maintain their freshness and beauty in the arrangement.

Arranging the flowers involves careful placement to achieve balance and harmony. Begin with a base of greenery to provide structure and support. Add the miniature roses in clusters or evenly spaced throughout the arrangement, depending on the desired look. Fill in with complementary flowers and foliage, paying attention to varying heights and textures to create a dynamic and layered effect. Using floral foam or a floral frog can help secure the stems and keep the arrangement in place.

Using miniature roses in floral arrangements offers versatility in design. They can be used in traditional, formal arrangements or more contemporary, free-form styles. For a romantic and timeless bouquet, combine pale pink and white roses with delicate baby's breath and trailing ivy. For a modern and bold look, mix brightly colored roses with unique foliage like monstera leaves or succulents. The versatility of miniature roses allows for endless creativity and personalization in floral design.

Maintaining the arrangement is essential for prolonging its beauty. Place the arrangement in a cool, well-lit area away from direct sunlight, drafts, and ripening fruits, which can release ethylene gas and shorten the life of the flowers. Change the water every two days, trim the stems slightly each time, and add fresh floral preservative to keep the flowers hydrated and healthy. Regular maintenance ensures that the arrangement remains fresh and vibrant for as long as possible.

Miniature roses also lend themselves well to other decorative uses beyond traditional arrangements. They can be incorporated into wreaths, garlands, and even wearable floral accessories like corsages and boutonnieres. Their compact size and delicate appearance make them ideal for adding a touch of elegance to a variety of decorative items. Exploring different ways to use miniature roses in floral design can enhance their appreciation and showcase their beauty in new and creative ways.

Chapter 10

Troubleshooting Common Issues

Yellowing Leaves and Their Causes

Yellowing leaves on miniature roses can indicate various underlying issues, ranging from nutrient deficiencies to pest infestations. One of the most common causes of yellowing leaves is a lack of essential nutrients, particularly nitrogen. Nitrogen is crucial for healthy leaf growth and chlorophyll production, and its deficiency can lead to pale, yellow leaves that eventually drop off. Addressing this issue involves applying a balanced fertilizer that includes nitrogen, ensuring the plants receive adequate nutrition for vigorous growth.

Overwatering or poor drainage can also cause yellowing leaves. When the soil is excessively wet, the roots may become waterlogged and unable to absorb oxygen, leading to root rot and nutrient deficiencies. Ensuring proper drainage and adjusting the watering schedule to allow the soil to dry out between waterings can prevent this issue. Using well-draining soil and containers with sufficient drainage holes helps maintain the right moisture balance for healthy root development.

Underwatering is another potential cause of yellowing leaves, as it leads to dehydration and stress in the plant. When miniature roses do not receive enough water, they may start to lose their lower leaves as a survival mechanism. Ensuring consistent and adequate watering, especially during hot and dry periods, is essential for maintaining the health and vitality of the roses. Monitoring soil moisture and watering deeply and regularly supports the plants' hydration needs.

Pest infestations can contribute to yellowing leaves by damaging the plant tissues and disrupting nutrient uptake. Common rose pests, such as aphids, spider mites, and thrips, feed on the sap and can cause leaves to yellow, curl, and drop prematurely. Regularly inspecting the plants for signs of pests and using appropriate control measures, such as insecticidal soap or neem oil, can help manage infestations and protect the health of the roses. Maintaining good garden hygiene and encouraging beneficial insects also support pest management.

Fungal diseases, such as black spot and powdery mildew, can cause yellowing leaves as well. Black spot appears as dark, circular spots with yellow halos, leading to leaf drop, while powdery mildew causes a white, powdery coating on the leaves and stems. Preventing and managing these diseases involves proper spacing, good air circulation, and regular pruning to remove infected plant material. Applying fungicides and maintaining a clean garden environment helps control fungal infections and reduce leaf yellowing.

Environmental stressors, such as extreme temperatures, can impact the health of miniature roses and cause yellowing leaves. High heat and intense sunlight can lead to sunburn and dehydration, while cold temperatures can cause frost damage. Providing shade during the hottest part of the day, ensuring adequate watering, and protecting the plants from frost can mitigate these stressors. Monitoring weather conditions and adapting care practices accordingly helps maintain the plants' health and resilience.

Root-bound plants, which occur when the roots outgrow their container, can also exhibit yellowing leaves due to restricted root space and nutrient uptake. Repotting the miniature roses into larger containers with fresh soil can alleviate this issue, allowing the roots to spread and access more nutrients. Regularly checking the root system and repotting as needed ensures that the plants have sufficient space for healthy growth and development.

Poor Bloom Production

Poor bloom production in miniature roses can be frustrating for gardeners, as it diminishes the plant's overall aesthetic appeal. One of the primary reasons for poor blooming is inadequate sunlight. Roses require at least six hours of direct sunlight each day to produce abundant blooms. Insufficient light can result in weak growth and fewer flowers. Ensuring that the roses are planted in a sunny location or providing supplemental lighting for indoor plants can enhance bloom production and overall plant health.

Nutrient deficiencies, particularly in phosphorus, can lead to reduced blooming. Phosphorus is essential for flower development and root growth, and a deficiency can result in fewer and smaller blooms. Applying a balanced fertilizer with a higher phosphorus content, such as a bloom booster, can promote flower production. Regular soil testing and appropriate fertilization ensure that the roses receive the necessary nutrients for optimal blooming.

Improper pruning practices can also affect bloom production. Over-pruning or incorrect timing can remove potential flowering canes and reduce the number of blooms. Pruning should be done in early spring, removing dead, damaged, or weak wood and shaping the plant to encourage healthy growth. Ensuring that the pruning cuts are made just above outward-facing buds promotes new growth and increases the chances of abundant blooming.

Environmental stressors, such as extreme temperatures or drought, can hinder bloom production. High temperatures can cause flower buds to drop or blooms to fade quickly, while drought stress can lead to poor growth and reduced flowering. Providing adequate water during dry periods, using mulch to retain soil moisture, and protecting the plants from extreme heat can mitigate these stressors. Ensuring a stable and supportive environment helps the roses produce healthy and abundant blooms.

Pests and diseases can also impact bloom production by damaging the buds and flowers. Pests such as thrips and Japanese beetles can feed on the flower buds, causing them to deform or fail to open. Fungal diseases like botrytis blight can cause the buds to rot. Regular monitoring, early detection, and appropriate pest and disease management practices can protect the blooms and support healthy flower development. Maintaining a clean garden environment and practicing good hygiene further reduce the risk of infestations and infections.

Inadequate watering practices can lead to poor bloom production. Both overwatering and underwatering can stress the plants and affect their ability to produce flowers. Ensuring consistent and adequate watering, especially during the blooming season, supports healthy growth and flower development. Deep watering that reaches the root zone encourages strong root systems and promotes blooming. Monitoring soil moisture and adjusting the watering schedule based on weather conditions and plant needs ensures optimal hydration.

Age and health of the rose plant can also influence bloom production. Older plants may produce fewer blooms as they age, and unhealthy plants weakened by stress or poor care are less likely to bloom abundantly. Regular maintenance, including feeding, watering, pruning, and monitoring for pests and diseases, helps maintain the health and vigor of the roses. Ensuring that the plants receive the necessary care and attention supports their ability to produce beautiful and plentiful blooms.

Addressing Wilting and Drooping

Wilting and drooping in miniature roses are common signs of stress, indicating that the plants are struggling with environmental or physiological issues. One of the primary causes of wilting is water stress, either due to underwatering or overwatering. Underwatered roses lack sufficient moisture to support their tissues, leading to wilting leaves and stems. Ensuring consistent and adequate watering, especially during hot and dry periods, helps prevent wilting. Deep watering that reaches the root zone supports healthy hydration and root development.

Conversely, overwatering can cause wilting by leading to waterlogged soil and root rot. When the roots are deprived of oxygen due to excess water, they cannot absorb nutrients and water effectively, resulting in wilting. Ensuring proper drainage in the soil and containers, reducing the frequency of watering, and allowing the soil to dry out between waterings can prevent overwatering. Monitoring soil moisture and adjusting the watering schedule based on environmental conditions helps maintain the right moisture balance.

Transplant shock can also cause wilting and drooping in newly planted or repotted miniature roses. The disturbance to the root system during transplanting can temporarily disrupt water and nutrient uptake, leading to stress. Providing adequate water, reducing direct sunlight, and applying a root stimulant can help the plants recover from transplant shock. Ensuring gentle handling and minimizing root disturbance during the transplant process supports a smoother transition and reduces the risk of wilting.

Temperature extremes, particularly high heat, can cause wilting as the plants lose water faster than they can absorb it. Providing shade during the hottest part of the day, increasing watering frequency, and using mulch to retain soil moisture can help mitigate heat stress. Protecting the plants from sudden temperature fluctuations and ensuring a stable environment supports their overall health and reduces wilting. Monitoring weather conditions and adapting care practices accordingly helps the roses cope with temperature stress.

Nutrient deficiencies, particularly in potassium, can lead to wilting and weak growth. Potassium is essential for regulating water movement within the plant and supporting overall vigor. Applying a balanced fertilizer that includes potassium can address deficiencies and improve plant health. Regular soil testing and appropriate fertilization ensure that the roses receive the necessary nutrients for robust growth and resilience.

Maintaining balanced nutrition supports the plants' ability to manage water stress and reduces wilting.

Pests and diseases can also contribute to wilting and drooping by damaging the plant tissues and disrupting nutrient and water uptake. Root-feeding pests, such as nematodes, can damage the roots and impair their function. Above-ground pests, like aphids and spider mites, can weaken the plants by feeding on their sap. Regularly inspecting the plants for signs of pests and diseases and using appropriate control measures can help manage these issues. Maintaining good garden hygiene and encouraging beneficial insects support pest management and plant health.

Structural issues, such as damage to the stems or root system, can cause wilting and drooping. Physical injury from pruning, high winds, or mechanical damage can disrupt the plant's vascular system, leading to wilting. Ensuring proper support for the plants, protecting them from physical damage, and providing gentle care can prevent structural issues. Regularly checking the plants for signs of damage and addressing any issues promptly supports their health and reduces the risk of wilting and drooping.

Chapter 11

Enhancing Bloom Quality and Longevity

Techniques for Bigger Blooms

Improving the Quality and Longevity of Miniature Rose Blooms

Achieving larger blooms on miniature roses involves a combination of pruning, feeding, and care techniques. One of the most effective methods is selective pruning, which directs the plant's energy towards fewer blooms. This process, known as disbudding, involves removing some of the smaller or less desirable buds early in the growing season. By focusing the plant's resources on a smaller number of buds, the remaining blooms can develop more fully and achieve greater size.

Feeding is another critical factor in promoting larger blooms. Providing a balanced fertilizer that is high in phosphorus supports the development of strong roots and large flowers. Phosphorus is essential for energy transfer and storage within the plant, which directly impacts bloom size and quality. Regularly applying a bloom booster fertilizer can enhance flower production. Organic options like bone meal or fish emulsion can also provide a slow-release source of phosphorus and other essential nutrients.

Watering practices play a significant role in bloom development. Consistent and deep watering ensures that the plants have sufficient moisture to support robust growth and large blooms. Deep watering encourages the development of a deep and extensive root system, which in turn supports healthy top growth and bloom formation. Avoiding fluctuations in soil moisture levels helps prevent stress, which can negatively impact bloom size and overall plant health.

Proper light exposure is crucial for achieving large blooms. Miniature roses require at least six hours of direct sunlight daily to produce strong, healthy flowers. Ensuring that the plants are placed in a sunny location maximizes their photosynthetic capacity, leading to better growth and larger blooms. In areas with intense sunlight, providing some afternoon shade can help prevent heat stress while still allowing for adequate light exposure.

Deadheading, or the removal of spent blooms, is important for maintaining bloom quality and encouraging continuous flowering. Deadheading prevents the plant from expending energy on seed production and instead redirects it towards new bud formation. Regularly removing faded flowers keeps the plant looking tidy and promotes the growth of larger, more vibrant blooms. Using clean, sharp tools for deadheading minimizes damage and reduces the risk of disease transmission.

Soil health and structure significantly impact bloom quality. Ensuring that the soil is well-draining and rich in organic matter provides a supportive environment for root growth. Incorporating compost or well-rotted manure into the soil enhances its fertility and structure, allowing roots to access nutrients more efficiently. Maintaining optimal soil conditions supports the overall health of the plants, leading to better bloom development.

Monitoring for pests and diseases is essential for protecting bloom quality. Pests such as aphids, thrips, and spider mites can damage buds and flowers, reducing their size and appearance. Regularly inspecting the plants and using appropriate control measures helps prevent infestations and protect the blooms. Fungicidal treatments may be necessary to manage diseases like black spot and powdery mildew, which can also affect bloom quality. Ensuring that the plants remain healthy and free from stressors is key to achieving large, high-quality blooms.

Extending Blooming Period

Extending the blooming period of miniature roses involves a combination of cultural practices, careful selection of rose varieties, and environmental management. One of the most effective ways to prolong the blooming season is through deadheading. Removing spent blooms encourages the plant to produce new flowers instead of diverting energy into seed production. Regular deadheading throughout the growing season can significantly extend the period during which the roses remain in bloom.

Selecting varieties known for their repeat blooming characteristics is essential for a prolonged blooming period. Some miniature roses are bred to produce flowers continuously or in multiple flushes throughout the growing season. Researching and choosing these varieties can ensure that the garden remains vibrant with color for an extended time. Varieties like 'Fairy', 'Beehive', and 'Magic Carrousel' are examples of repeat bloomers that can provide continuous interest.

Providing consistent and appropriate care is crucial for maintaining a prolonged blooming period. This includes regular feeding with a balanced fertilizer that supports ongoing growth and flower production. Using a fertilizer high in potassium can enhance bloom longevity and overall plant vigor. Applying a liquid fertilizer every four to six weeks during the growing season ensures that the plants receive a steady supply of nutrients to support continuous blooming.

Watering practices directly impact the length of the blooming period. Ensuring that the roses receive consistent moisture without becoming waterlogged supports healthy growth and bloom production. Deep, thorough watering encourages strong root development and helps the plants withstand periods of drought. Mulching around the base of the plants can help retain soil moisture and regulate temperature, creating a more stable growing environment that supports prolonged blooming.

Pruning practices can also influence the blooming period. Light pruning throughout the season can help maintain plant shape and encourage new growth. Removing old or weak canes and thinning out overcrowded areas improves air circulation and light penetration, which can enhance bloom production. Strategic pruning at the right times can stimulate new flushes of growth and flowers, extending the overall blooming period.

Environmental factors such as temperature and light play a significant role in bloom duration. Providing some shade during the hottest part of the day can prevent heat stress and prolong the life of the blooms. In regions with long growing seasons, protecting the plants from extreme weather conditions can help maintain continuous bloom production. Using shade cloths, windbreaks, or other protective measures can mitigate environmental stressors and support prolonged flowering.

Regular monitoring and pest management are essential for maintaining a prolonged blooming period. Pests and diseases can quickly reduce bloom quality and shorten the blooming season. Implementing an integrated pest management (IPM) approach that includes regular inspections, cultural practices, and organic treatments can keep pest populations under control. Ensuring that the plants remain healthy and free from stressors supports continuous bloom production and extends the enjoyment of the roses throughout the growing season.

Using Growth Regulators

Growth regulators are specialized chemicals used to influence plant growth and development, and they can be particularly useful in enhancing bloom quality and longevity in miniature roses. These substances can promote or inhibit specific growth processes, depending on the desired outcome. One common type of growth regulator used in rose cultivation is gibberellic acid, which can stimulate cell elongation and increase flower size.

Applying gibberellic acid in appropriate doses can result in larger, more impressive blooms.

Another beneficial growth regulator is cytokinin, which promotes cell division and delays aging in plant tissues. Cytokinins can be used to prolong the life of rose blooms by slowing down the senescence process. This results in flowers that remain fresh and vibrant for a longer period. Applying cytokinin-based products during the flowering stage can enhance bloom longevity and improve the overall aesthetic of the roses. Ensuring correct application rates and timing is crucial for achieving the desired effects without causing harm to the plants.

Ethylene inhibitors are growth regulators that can prevent the negative effects of ethylene, a natural plant hormone that accelerates aging and flower drop. Using products that inhibit ethylene production or action can help extend the life of rose blooms, especially during stressful conditions such as high temperatures or transportation. These inhibitors are particularly useful in maintaining the quality of cut flowers, ensuring they remain attractive for an extended period. Integrating ethylene inhibitors into the care routine can enhance the overall performance of miniature roses.

Auxins are another group of growth regulators that can influence rooting and shoot growth. While auxins are commonly used for rooting cuttings, they can also be applied to promote uniform growth and improve the structure of rose plants. Using auxin-based products to encourage strong root development supports the plant's ability to uptake water and nutrients, leading to healthier growth and more prolific blooming. Balancing auxin levels in the plant can enhance overall growth and bloom quality.

It is important to note that the use of growth regulators requires careful consideration and precise application. Overuse or incorrect application can lead to undesirable effects, such as distorted growth or reduced plant vigor. Following manufacturer guidelines and conducting small-scale tests before widespread application can help ensure the best results. Understanding the specific needs and growth patterns of miniature roses allows for the effective use of growth regulators to enhance bloom quality and longevity.

Combining growth regulators with other cultural practices can maximize their benefits. For example, applying growth regulators in conjunction with proper fertilization, watering, and pruning routines can create an optimal growing environment for the roses. Integrating these substances into a comprehensive care plan supports the overall health and performance of the plants. Regular monitoring and adjustment of growth regulator applications based on plant response help achieve the desired outcomes.

While growth regulators can significantly enhance bloom quality and longevity, they should be used as part of an integrated approach to rose care. Ensuring that the basic needs of the plants are met, including adequate sunlight, water, and nutrition, provides a strong foundation for the effective use of these substances. Combining growth regulators with sound horticultural practices creates an environment where miniature roses can thrive and produce exceptional blooms.

Chapter 12

Water Management

Efficient Watering Systems

Efficient watering systems are essential for maintaining the health and vigor of miniature roses while conserving water resources. One of the most effective systems for rose gardens is drip irrigation. This method delivers water directly to the root zone of each plant through a network of tubing and emitters. Drip irrigation minimizes water loss due to evaporation and runoff, ensuring that the plants receive a consistent and adequate supply of moisture. The system can be automated with timers, allowing for precise control over watering schedules and reducing the labor involved in hand-watering.

Another efficient watering system is the soaker hose, which is similar to drip irrigation but uses a porous hose that releases water along its length. Soaker hoses can be laid out along rows of plants or wound around individual rose bushes. This method provides deep, even watering that encourages strong root development and reduces water waste. Soaker hoses are particularly useful in areas with dense plantings, where overhead watering would be less effective and could promote disease.

Automated sprinkler systems, while less efficient than drip or soaker hoses, can still be optimized for water conservation and effective irrigation. Sprinkler heads should be adjusted to deliver water evenly and at the appropriate rate for the soil and plant types. Using low-angle or rotary nozzles can reduce water loss due to wind drift and evaporation.

Additionally, scheduling watering sessions for early morning or late evening minimizes evaporation and allows the water to penetrate the soil before the heat of the day.

Rainwater harvesting systems can complement traditional watering methods by providing a sustainable source of irrigation water. Collecting rainwater in barrels or cisterns and using it to water the roses can reduce reliance on municipal water supplies and lower water bills. Rainwater is also free of chlorine and other chemicals commonly found in tap water, making it beneficial for the plants. Integrating rainwater harvesting with drip or soaker systems can create a highly efficient and environmentally friendly watering setup.

Soil moisture sensors are valuable tools for managing water usage and ensuring that plants receive the right amount of water. These sensors can be placed in the soil at various depths to monitor moisture levels and provide real-time data. Connecting soil moisture sensors to an automated irrigation system allows for precise adjustments based on actual soil conditions, preventing overwatering or underwatering. This technology helps maintain optimal soil moisture levels, promoting healthy plant growth and reducing water waste.

Mulching is an important practice that complements efficient watering systems. Applying a layer of organic mulch, such as wood chips, straw, or compost, around the base of the roses helps retain soil moisture, reduce evaporation, and regulate soil temperature. Mulch also suppresses weeds, which can compete with the roses for water and nutrients. Maintaining a consistent mulch layer throughout the growing season enhances the effectiveness of the watering system and supports overall plant health.

Regular maintenance and monitoring of the watering system are crucial for ensuring its efficiency and effectiveness. Checking for leaks, clogs, and other issues in the irrigation lines or hoses helps prevent water waste and ensures that all plants receive adequate moisture. Adjusting the watering schedule based on seasonal changes and weather conditions ensures that the roses receive the right amount of water throughout the year. A well-maintained and efficiently managed watering system is key to the success of miniature rose gardening.

Mulching for Moisture Retention

Mulching is a highly effective practice for retaining soil moisture and promoting the health of miniature roses. Applying a layer of mulch around the base of the plants helps reduce evaporation, conserve water, and maintain consistent soil moisture levels. Organic mulches, such as wood chips, straw, compost, or shredded leaves, are particularly beneficial as they decompose over time, adding nutrients to the soil and improving its structure. Mulch acts as an insulating layer, protecting the roots from extreme temperature fluctuations and reducing soil erosion.

One of the primary benefits of mulching is its ability to suppress weed growth. Weeds compete with roses for water, nutrients, and light, and can significantly impact their health and growth. A thick layer of mulch effectively blocks sunlight from reaching weed seeds, preventing their germination and growth. This reduces the need for frequent weeding and allows the roses to thrive without competition. Maintaining a mulch layer of 2 to 3 inches thick ensures effective weed suppression and moisture retention.

Mulch also plays a crucial role in regulating soil temperature. During hot weather, mulch keeps the soil cooler by shading it from direct sunlight, reducing heat stress on the roots. In cold weather, mulch acts as an insulating layer, protecting the roots from freezing temperatures and preventing frost heaving. This temperature regulation supports consistent root growth and overall plant health, helping the roses withstand environmental stressors.

As organic mulch decomposes, it enriches the soil with valuable nutrients, improving soil fertility and structure. The decomposition process enhances microbial activity in the soil, promoting a healthy and balanced soil ecosystem. This increased microbial activity helps break down organic matter, releasing nutrients that are readily available to the plants. Incorporating mulch into the soil over time improves its water-holding capacity and drainage, creating an optimal growing environment for the roses.

Applying mulch correctly is essential for maximizing its benefits. The mulch should be spread evenly around the base of the plants, extending out to the drip line but not touching the stems. Mulch piled against the stems can retain moisture and create a favorable environment for pests and diseases. Maintaining a gap between the mulch and the stems ensures proper air circulation and reduces the risk of rot and fungal infections.

Regularly replenishing the mulch layer as it decomposes ensures continued benefits.

Different types of mulch offer various advantages, and choosing the right mulch depends on specific garden needs and preferences. Wood chips and bark mulch are long-lasting and provide excellent weed suppression and moisture retention. Straw and hay decompose more quickly, adding organic matter to the soil but requiring more frequent replenishment. Compost and shredded leaves break down rapidly, enriching the soil with nutrients but also needing regular replenishment. Understanding the characteristics of each mulch type helps in selecting the most suitable option for the garden.

Incorporating mulch into the overall garden care routine enhances its effectiveness. Combining mulching with efficient watering systems, proper fertilization, and regular pruning supports the health and vigor of the roses. Monitoring the garden and adjusting care practices based on seasonal changes and plant needs ensures optimal growth and blooming. Mulching is a simple yet powerful practice that significantly contributes to the success and beauty of miniature rose gardens.

Recognizing Water Stress

Recognizing water stress in miniature roses is crucial for maintaining their health and preventing long-term damage. Water stress occurs when the plants do not receive adequate moisture to support their physiological processes, leading to symptoms such as wilting, yellowing leaves, and reduced growth. One of the most apparent signs of water stress is wilting, where the leaves and stems lose turgor pressure and appear droopy. This condition indicates that the plant is unable to maintain adequate hydration and requires immediate attention.

Yellowing leaves, particularly those starting from the bottom of the plant, can also indicate water stress. While yellowing can result from other issues such as nutrient deficiencies or diseases, it often signifies that the roots are not receiving enough water. Inconsistent watering, where the soil alternates between being too dry and too wet, can exacerbate this problem. Ensuring a consistent and adequate watering schedule helps prevent yellowing leaves due to water stress.

Stunted growth and reduced blooming are additional symptoms of water stress. When plants do not receive enough water, they prioritize survival over growth and reproduction, leading to smaller leaves, shorter stems, and fewer flowers. Monitoring the overall growth and vigor of the plants can help identify water stress early. Providing sufficient water during critical growth periods, such as bud formation and flowering, supports healthy development and abundant blooms.

Crispy or brown leaf edges can also be a sign of water stress, particularly in hot and dry conditions. This occurs when the plant loses more water through transpiration than it can absorb from the soil, leading to localized dehydration. Ensuring deep and thorough watering, especially during heatwaves, helps prevent this symptom. Using mulch to retain soil moisture and providing shade during the hottest part of the day can also mitigate heat-related water stress.

Soil moisture levels are a direct indicator of water availability to the plants. Regularly checking the soil moisture using a moisture meter or simply feeling the soil can help determine if the plants are receiving adequate water. The soil should be moist but not waterlogged, and the top inch should be allowed to dry out slightly between waterings. Maintaining optimal soil moisture levels supports healthy root function and prevents water stress.

Understanding the specific water needs of miniature roses helps in preventing water stress. These plants generally require about 1 to 2 inches of water per week, depending on weather conditions and soil type. Sandy soils may require more frequent watering due to their quick drainage, while clay soils may need less frequent watering but deeper irrigation to penetrate the dense soil. Adjusting the watering schedule based on soil type and environmental conditions ensures that the plants receive adequate hydration.

Preventing water stress involves a combination of proper watering practices, soil management, and environmental protection. Using efficient watering systems, such as drip irrigation or soaker hoses, ensures that water is delivered directly to the root zone with minimal waste. Mulching helps retain soil moisture and regulate temperature, reducing the risk of water stress. Monitoring weather conditions and adjusting care practices accordingly ensures that the roses remain healthy and resilient, free from the detrimental effects of water stress.

Chapter 13

Soil Health and Fertility

Organic Soil Amendments

Enhancing soil health and fertility through organic amendments is essential for the robust growth of miniature roses. Organic amendments improve soil structure, increase nutrient content, and support beneficial microbial activity. One of the most effective organic amendments is compost. Compost is rich in essential nutrients and beneficial microorganisms that enhance soil fertility and structure. It improves water retention in sandy soils and drainage in clay soils, creating an ideal growing environment for roses.

Well-rotted manure is another excellent organic amendment. It provides a slow-release source of nutrients, including nitrogen, phosphorus, and potassium, which are vital for plant growth. Manure also enhances soil microbial activity, promoting a healthy soil ecosystem. It is important to use well-composted manure to avoid burning the plants and to minimize the risk of introducing weed seeds and pathogens.

Bone meal, derived from ground animal bones, is a valuable source of phosphorus and calcium. These nutrients are crucial for root development and flower production. Bone meal releases nutrients slowly, making it an excellent long-term amendment for soil fertility. Incorporating bone meal into the soil before planting can significantly improve the growth and bloom quality of miniature roses.

Blood meal, a byproduct of the meatpacking industry, is a high-nitrogen organic fertilizer. Nitrogen is essential for healthy leaf and stem growth. Blood meal provides a quick-release source of nitrogen, making it ideal for correcting nitrogen deficiencies and promoting vigorous growth. However, it should be used sparingly to avoid over-fertilization, which can lead to excessive foliage growth at the expense of blooms.

Seaweed extract is another beneficial organic amendment. It is rich in micronutrients, such as magnesium, potassium, and trace elements, which are essential for overall plant health. Seaweed also contains growth hormones that stimulate root development and enhance stress tolerance. Applying seaweed extract as a soil drench or foliar spray can boost the health and resilience of miniature roses.

Green manure crops, such as clover, alfalfa, and rye, can be grown and then turned into the soil to improve its fertility and structure. These cover crops add organic matter, improve soil texture, and enhance nutrient availability. They also help suppress weeds and prevent soil erosion. Growing green manure crops in rotation with roses can significantly improve soil health over time.

Mycorrhizal fungi are beneficial soil organisms that form symbiotic relationships with plant roots. These fungi enhance nutrient and water uptake, improve soil structure, and increase plant resilience to environmental stressors. Inoculating the soil with mycorrhizal fungi can boost the growth and health of miniature roses. Mycorrhizal inoculants are available in various forms, including powders and granules, and can be applied directly to the soil or as a root dip during planting.

Composting Tips

Adding compost to miniature roses to enhance soil quality

Composting is an effective way to recycle organic waste into a nutrient-rich soil amendment. Starting with a balanced mix of green and brown materials is crucial for successful composting. Green materials, such as grass clippings, vegetable scraps, and coffee grounds, provide nitrogen, while brown materials, like leaves, straw, and cardboard, supply carbon. Maintaining a ratio of roughly three parts brown to one part green helps create a well-balanced compost.

Aeration is vital for the composting process. Turning the compost pile regularly ensures that oxygen is evenly distributed, which accelerates decomposition and prevents the pile from becoming anaerobic. An anaerobic compost pile can emit unpleasant odors and slow down the composting process. Using a pitchfork or compost turner to mix the pile every few weeks helps maintain proper aeration and speeds up the breakdown of materials.

Moisture is another critical factor in composting. The compost pile should be kept as moist as a wrung-out sponge. If the pile is too dry, decomposition will slow down; if it is too wet, it can become compacted and anaerobic. Adding water during dry periods and covering the pile with a tarp during heavy rain helps maintain the right moisture balance. Regularly checking the moisture level and adjusting as needed ensures optimal composting conditions.

Chopping or shredding compost materials into smaller pieces can significantly speed up the composting process. Smaller pieces have a larger surface area for microbial activity, which enhances decomposition. Using a garden shredder or simply chopping materials with a shovel or pruners before adding them to the pile helps create a finer and more homogeneous compost.

Adding compost activators can also enhance the composting process. Compost activators contain high levels of nitrogen and beneficial microorganisms that kickstart decomposition. Common activators include fresh grass clippings, manure, and alfalfa meal. Adding these materials in thin layers throughout the pile can boost microbial activity and accelerate composting.

Monitoring the temperature of the compost pile provides insights into its progress. A healthy compost pile will heat up to 120-160°F (49-71°C) during active decomposition. Using a compost thermometer to check the temperature regularly helps ensure that the pile is decomposing properly. If the pile cools down prematurely, it may need more turning, water, or nitrogen-rich materials to reheat.

Patience is essential when composting. The composting process can take several months to a year, depending on the materials used and the management of the pile. Finished compost should be dark, crumbly, and have an earthy smell. Sifting the compost through a screen can remove any remaining large pieces, ensuring a fine and uniform final product. Properly finished compost is a valuable soil amendment that enhances soil fertility, structure, and microbial activity.

Soil Testing and Analysis

Soil testing and analysis are fundamental practices for understanding soil health and fertility. Conducting a soil test provides valuable information about the nutrient content, pH level, and overall condition of the soil. This data helps gardeners make informed decisions about fertilization, soil amendments, and other management practices. Collecting soil samples from different areas of the garden ensures a comprehensive analysis of the soil's condition.

When collecting soil samples, it is important to use clean tools and follow proper sampling techniques. Soil samples should be taken from the root zone, typically 6-8 inches deep, using a soil probe or garden trowel. Mixing samples from several locations within the same area provides a representative composite sample. Placing the samples in a clean container and allowing them to air dry before testing prevents contamination and ensures accurate results.

Sending soil samples to a reputable laboratory for analysis provides detailed information about nutrient levels and soil pH. Laboratory tests measure the concentration of essential nutrients, such as nitrogen, phosphorus, potassium, calcium, magnesium, and trace elements. The results are typically presented in an easy-to-understand report that includes recommendations for fertilization and soil amendments based on the test findings.

Interpreting soil test results involves understanding the nutrient levels and pH requirements of the plants being grown. Miniature roses thrive in slightly acidic to neutral soil with a pH range of 6.0-7.0. If the soil pH is outside this range, amendments such as lime (to raise pH) or sulfur (to lower pH) can be applied to adjust it. Balancing soil pH is essential for nutrient availability and overall plant health.

Based on the soil test results, specific fertilizers and amendments can be selected to address nutrient deficiencies or imbalances. For example, if the soil is deficient in phosphorus, applying bone meal or a phosphorus-rich fertilizer can enhance bloom production. If potassium levels are low, incorporating potash or potassium sulfate can improve overall plant vigor. Tailoring fertilization practices to the specific needs of the soil ensures optimal nutrient availability for the roses.

Regular soil testing, ideally every 2-3 years, helps track changes in soil health and fertility over time. Monitoring trends in nutrient levels and pH allows for adjustments to be made as needed, preventing nutrient deficiencies or toxicities. Keeping records of soil test results and management practices provides a valuable reference for future gardening decisions. Consistent soil testing and analysis are key to maintaining healthy and fertile soil for miniature roses.

Understanding soil texture and structure is also important for soil health and fertility. Conducting a simple soil texture test, such as the jar test or ribbon test, helps determine the proportions of sand, silt, and clay in the soil. Soil structure can be improved by incorporating organic matter, which enhances water retention, drainage, and root penetration.

Chapter 14

Companion Planting and Biodiversity

Beneficial Companion Plants

Miniature roses with companion plants such as yarrow, calendula, and marigold

Companion planting is a gardening technique that involves growing different plant species together to enhance growth, repel pests, and improve soil health. Miniature roses can benefit significantly from the strategic use of companion plants. One of the most effective companion plants for roses is lavender. Lavender's strong scent helps deter aphids and other common rose pests, while its flowers attract beneficial insects like bees and predatory wasps. Additionally, lavender's low water requirements and similar sun preferences make it an ideal companion for roses.

Marigolds are another excellent companion plant for roses. They secrete a substance from their roots that repels nematodes, which can damage rose roots. Marigolds also attract pollinators and other beneficial insects, such as ladybugs and hoverflies, that help control aphid populations. Planting marigolds around the base of rose bushes can create a protective barrier against pests while adding vibrant color to the garden.

Chives and garlic are valuable companion plants for roses due to their pest-repellent properties. The strong odor of these alliums deters aphids, Japanese beetles, and other pests. Additionally, they can help prevent fungal diseases like black spot and powdery mildew by emitting sulfur compounds. Interplanting chives or garlic with roses can enhance the health and resilience of the rose bushes.

Catmint (Nepeta) is another beneficial companion for roses. Its aromatic foliage repels aphids, Japanese beetles, and other pests, while its flowers attract pollinators and beneficial insects. Catmint's sprawling habit can also serve as a living mulch, helping to retain soil moisture and suppress weeds. Planting catmint near roses creates a mutually beneficial relationship that enhances the overall health of the garden.

Yarrow (Achillea) is a valuable companion plant for roses, known for its ability to attract beneficial insects such as ladybugs, lacewings, and parasitic wasps. These insects prey on common rose pests, helping to keep their populations in check. Yarrow also improves soil health by accumulating nutrients and making them more available to nearby plants. Incorporating yarrow into rose plantings can boost biodiversity and support a balanced garden ecosystem.

Borage (Borago officinalis) is another excellent companion for roses. Its blue flowers attract pollinators and beneficial insects, while its deep roots help break up compacted soil and improve drainage. Borage is also known to enhance the flavor and growth of nearby plants through allelopathy, a natural phenomenon where certain plants release chemicals that benefit other plants. Growing borage near roses can enhance their growth and bloom quality.

Calendula, also known as pot marigold, is a beneficial companion plant that repels a variety of pests, including aphids, thrips, and whiteflies. Its bright flowers attract pollinators and predatory insects, supporting a healthy garden ecosystem. Calendula's roots also secrete substances that improve soil health and structure. Planting calendula with roses adds aesthetic appeal and contributes to the overall health and resilience of the garden.

Creating a Balanced Ecosystem

Creating a balanced ecosystem in the garden involves fostering biodiversity and encouraging beneficial relationships between plants, insects, and soil organisms. One of the foundational practices is to plant a diverse array of species that can support each other and attract beneficial wildlife. Using a mix of flowering plants, herbs, shrubs, and ground covers creates a rich tapestry that enhances the garden's resilience and productivity.

Encouraging native plants is an effective way to support local biodiversity. Native plants are well-adapted to the local climate and soil conditions, making them low-maintenance and beneficial for the ecosystem. They provide food and habitat for native pollinators, birds, and other wildlife.

Incorporating native plants into the garden alongside roses can create a harmonious and sustainable environment that supports a wide range of species.

Providing habitat for beneficial insects is crucial for maintaining a balanced ecosystem. Insect hotels, brush piles, and undisturbed garden areas offer shelter and breeding sites for predatory insects, pollinators, and other beneficial organisms. Encouraging these insects helps control pest populations naturally and supports pollination, which is vital for fruit and seed production. Creating a garden that welcomes beneficial insects enhances its health and resilience.

Maintaining healthy soil is fundamental for a balanced garden ecosystem. Using organic soil amendments, practicing crop rotation, and minimizing soil disturbance all contribute to soil health. Healthy soil teems with beneficial microorganisms that improve nutrient cycling, enhance plant growth, and suppress soil-borne diseases. Building and maintaining rich, living soil is a cornerstone of sustainable gardening and supports the entire garden ecosystem.

Water management is another critical aspect of creating a balanced ecosystem. Using efficient irrigation systems, such as drip irrigation or soaker hoses, conserves water and reduces the risk of fungal diseases. Rainwater harvesting systems can provide a sustainable source of irrigation water. Proper water management ensures that plants receive adequate moisture while minimizing water waste and supporting the garden's overall health.

Incorporating perennials and annuals with different blooming times ensures continuous food sources for pollinators and beneficial insects throughout the growing season. Plants that bloom in early spring, mid-summer, and late fall provide a steady supply of nectar and pollen, supporting a diverse population of pollinators. Designing the garden with overlapping bloom periods enhances its attractiveness to wildlife and supports a balanced ecosystem.

Practicing integrated pest management (IPM) is essential for maintaining a healthy garden ecosystem. IPM combines cultural practices, biological control, and, when necessary, organic or chemical interventions to manage pest populations. Regular monitoring, encouraging beneficial insects, and using targeted treatments help keep pest populations under control while minimizing harm to non-target species and the environment. Implementing IPM principles supports a balanced and resilient garden ecosystem.

Pest-Repellent Plants

Pest-repellent plants play a vital role in organic gardening by naturally deterring harmful insects and reducing the need for chemical pesticides. Planting pest-repellent species alongside roses can protect them from common pests and support a healthy garden environment. One of the most effective pest-repellent plants is the marigold. Marigolds release a strong scent that repels nematodes, aphids, and whiteflies. Their roots also produce chemicals that deter root-knot nematodes, making them an excellent companion for roses.

Basil is another valuable pest-repellent plant. Its aromatic leaves repel mosquitoes, flies, and aphids. Planting basil near roses can protect them from these pests while providing a fresh culinary herb. Basil's flowers also attract beneficial insects like bees and predatory wasps, further supporting pest control in the garden.

Rosemary is a robust herb that deters a variety of pests, including cabbage moths, bean beetles, and carrot flies. Its strong scent confuses and repels these pests, making it a useful companion plant. Rosemary's woody stems and evergreen foliage also add structural interest to the garden, and its flowers attract pollinators and beneficial insects. Integrating rosemary into rose plantings enhances pest control and adds aesthetic appeal.

Sage is known for its pest-repellent properties, particularly against cabbage moths, carrot flies, and flea beetles. The strong scent of sage leaves deters these pests, protecting nearby plants. Sage also attracts beneficial insects like bees and butterflies, supporting pollination and biodiversity. Planting sage around roses can create a protective barrier while adding visual and aromatic interest to the garden.

Thyme is another aromatic herb that repels various pests, including cabbage worms, whiteflies, and tomato hornworms. Its low-growing habit makes it an excellent ground cover, helping to suppress weeds and retain soil moisture. Thyme's flowers attract pollinators and predatory insects, contributing to a balanced garden ecosystem. Using thyme as a companion plant for roses provides pest control benefits and enhances the garden's overall health.

Mint is well-known for its strong scent, which repels ants, aphids, and flea beetles. However, mint can be invasive, so it is best grown in containers or confined areas to prevent it from spreading uncontrollably. Planting mint near roses in pots or designated garden beds can protect them from pests while providing a useful herb for culinary purposes. The flowers of mint also attract beneficial insects, supporting a healthy garden environment.

Alliums, including garlic, onions, and chives, are effective pest-repellent plants. Their pungent scent deters aphids, Japanese beetles, and carrot flies. Planting alliums near roses can create a protective barrier against these pests. Additionally, alliums have antimicrobial properties that can help prevent fungal diseases. Integrating alliums into the garden enhances pest control and supports the health of the roses.

Chapter 15

Sustainable and Eco-Friendly Practices

Reducing Chemical Use

Reducing chemical use in the garden is a fundamental aspect of sustainable and eco-friendly gardening. One effective way to minimize chemical use is through integrated pest management (IPM). IPM combines biological, cultural, mechanical, and chemical control methods to manage pests in the most environmentally friendly way possible. This approach prioritizes the use of natural predators, like ladybugs and lacewings, which feed on common rose pests such as aphids and spider mites. By encouraging these beneficial insects, gardeners can significantly reduce the need for chemical pesticides.

Cultural practices, such as crop rotation and proper plant spacing, can also help reduce chemical use. Rotating crops disrupts the life cycles of pests and diseases, while adequate spacing improves air circulation, reducing the risk of fungal infections. Implementing these practices creates a healthier growing environment, making plants less susceptible to pests and diseases, thereby reducing the need for chemical interventions.

Mechanical controls, such as handpicking pests or using barriers like row covers, provide another way to manage garden pests without chemicals. Regularly inspecting plants and removing pests manually can effectively keep populations under control. Using physical barriers to protect plants from insect pests further minimizes the need for chemical treatments. These methods are especially useful for managing larger pests and preventing damage from the outset.

Organic pesticides and fungicides, made from natural ingredients, offer an alternative to synthetic chemicals. Products like neem oil, insecticidal soap, and horticultural oils can effectively control pests and diseases without harming beneficial insects or the environment. These organic options decompose quickly and leave no harmful residues, making them a safer choice for both the garden and the gardener. Applying these products as needed rather than on a routine basis can also help reduce overall chemical use.

Soil health plays a crucial role in reducing the need for chemical fertilizers. Maintaining healthy, nutrient-rich soil through the use of organic amendments, such as compost and manure, supports robust plant growth and resilience. Healthy plants are better able to resist pests and diseases, reducing the need for chemical interventions. Regular soil testing and appropriate amendments ensure that plants receive the nutrients they need from natural sources.

Companion planting is another strategy to reduce chemical use. Certain plants can repel pests or attract beneficial insects, creating a more balanced and healthy garden ecosystem. For example, planting garlic or chives near roses can help deter aphids, while marigolds can repel nematodes. Integrating these companion plants into the garden reduces reliance on chemical pesticides and fosters a more sustainable gardening practice.

Educating oneself about sustainable gardening techniques is essential for reducing chemical use. Staying informed about the latest research and developments in organic and sustainable gardening practices empowers gardeners to make more eco-friendly choices. Joining gardening groups, attending workshops, and reading up-to-date literature can provide valuable insights and practical tips for maintaining a healthy garden without relying on synthetic chemicals.

Water Conservation Techniques

Implementing water conservation techniques is crucial for sustainable gardening and ensuring that miniature roses receive adequate moisture without wasting resources. Drip irrigation systems are among the most efficient methods for watering roses. These systems deliver water directly to the plant's root zone, minimizing evaporation and runoff. Drip irrigation systems can be set on timers to ensure consistent watering, providing the right amount of moisture at the right time and reducing water waste.

Mulching is another effective water conservation technique. Applying a layer of organic mulch, such as wood chips, straw, or compost, around the base of the roses helps retain soil moisture by reducing evaporation. Mulch also regulates soil temperature, suppresses weeds, and adds organic matter to the soil as it decomposes. Maintaining a mulch layer of 2 to 3 inches thick significantly improves water retention and reduces the need for frequent watering.

Rainwater harvesting is a sustainable way to collect and use natural rainfall for garden irrigation. Installing rain barrels or cisterns to capture rainwater from rooftops provides a free and eco-friendly source of water for roses. Using harvested rainwater reduces the demand on municipal water supplies and lowers water bills. Rainwater is also free of the chemicals and salts found in tap water, making it beneficial for plant health.

Hydrozoning, or grouping plants with similar water needs together, is an effective water conservation strategy. By planting roses with other drought-tolerant or water-efficient plants, gardeners can ensure that all plants in the area receive appropriate irrigation. This approach reduces water waste and ensures that plants are not over or under-watered. Hydrozoning simplifies watering routines and promotes more efficient use of water resources.

Using greywater systems to recycle household water for garden use is another innovative water conservation method. Greywater, which comes from sinks, showers, and washing machines (excluding water from toilets), can be safely used to irrigate non-edible plants, including roses. Installing a greywater system allows gardeners to reuse water that would otherwise go down the drain, significantly reducing overall water consumption. Ensuring that greywater is free of harmful chemicals and using it appropriately supports sustainable water use.

Smart irrigation controllers and soil moisture sensors can help optimize watering schedules and prevent overwatering. These devices monitor weather conditions, soil moisture levels, and plant needs to adjust irrigation accordingly. Smart controllers can be programmed to water only when necessary, based on real-time data, while soil moisture sensors provide precise information about when to water. Using technology to manage irrigation ensures efficient water use and promotes healthier plants.

Practicing deep and infrequent watering encourages deep root growth and drought tolerance in roses. Watering deeply but less frequently ensures that water penetrates the soil to the root zone, promoting strong root development. This method reduces water loss through evaporation and encourages plants to develop more resilient root systems. Adjusting watering practices to align with seasonal changes and weather conditions further enhances water conservation efforts in the garden.

Encouraging Wildlife

Encouraging wildlife in the garden promotes biodiversity and creates a balanced ecosystem that benefits both plants and animals. One of the most effective ways to attract wildlife is by providing a variety of native plants. Native plants offer food, shelter, and breeding sites for local wildlife, including birds, insects, and small mammals. Incorporating a diverse range of native plants into the garden supports a wide array of species and enhances the ecological health of the area.

Creating habitats for beneficial insects is crucial for a thriving garden ecosystem. Insect hotels, made from materials like bamboo, wood, and straw, provide shelter for pollinators, such as bees, and predatory insects, like ladybugs and lacewings. These structures can be placed throughout the garden to support insect populations. Beneficial insects play a vital role in pollination and pest control, reducing the need for chemical interventions and supporting plant health.

Birds are essential for controlling pests and pollinating plants. Providing bird feeders, bird baths, and nesting boxes encourages birds to visit and reside in the garden. Planting berry-producing shrubs and trees, such as elderberry and serviceberry, provides a natural food source for birds. Birds help control insect populations and disperse seeds, contributing to the garden's ecological balance and plant diversity.

Water features, such as ponds, fountains, or simple birdbaths, attract a variety of wildlife, including amphibians, insects, and birds. Ponds can support frogs and toads, which are effective pest controllers. Adding aquatic plants to ponds creates a balanced habitat for these species. Fountains and birdbaths provide essential drinking and bathing water for birds and insects. Maintaining clean water sources ensures that wildlife has access to fresh water throughout the year.

Butterflies and moths are important pollinators and can be attracted to the garden by planting nectar-rich flowers. Plants like butterfly bush, milkweed, and coneflower provide abundant nectar for these insects. Creating sunny, sheltered areas with diverse flowering plants supports the lifecycle of butterflies and moths, from egg to adult. Providing host plants for caterpillars, such as milkweed for monarchs, further encourages butterfly populations.

Leaving some areas of the garden wild or less manicured can create habitats for a variety of wildlife. Piles of leaves, brush, and logs provide shelter and breeding sites for small mammals, insects, and amphibians. Allowing some plants to go to seed and leaving fallen fruit on the ground offers food for wildlife. These practices enhance the garden's biodiversity and create a more resilient and self-sustaining ecosystem.

Reducing the use of pesticides and herbicides is critical for encouraging wildlife. Chemicals can harm beneficial insects, birds, and other wildlife, disrupting the ecological balance. Adopting organic and sustainable gardening practices supports a healthier environment for all species. Creating a garden that welcomes wildlife involves thoughtful planning and management, fostering a vibrant and diverse ecosystem that benefits both the garden and the natural world.

Chapter 16

Additional Chapter

Essential Terms Every Rose Gardener Should Know

- **Deadheading:** The process of removing spent or faded blooms to encourage new growth and continuous flowering.
- **Dormancy:** A period when the rose plant stops active growth, typically during winter, to conserve energy.
- **Pruning:** The practice of cutting back stems and branches to shape the plant, remove deadwood, and promote healthy growth.
- **Propagation:** The method of producing new miniature rose plants, commonly done through cuttings or layering.
- **Transplanting:** Moving a miniature rose plant from one location to another, often from a pot to the ground or a larger container.
- **Fertilizer:** Nutrient-rich substances added to the soil to provide essential elements like nitrogen, phosphorus, and potassium for healthy plant growth.
- **Pest Control:** Techniques used to manage or eliminate pests such as aphids, spider mites, or whiteflies that can damage miniature roses.
- **Hybridization:** The process of cross-breeding two different rose varieties to create a new cultivar with desirable traits.
- **Mulching:** Adding a protective layer of organic or inorganic material around the base of the plant to retain moisture, regulate soil temperature, and suppress weeds.

- **Soil pH:** The measure of acidity or alkalinity in the soil, with roses typically preferring slightly acidic soil (pH 6.0–6.5).
- **Rootstock:** The root system of a plant used in grafting to provide a sturdy base for the desired rose variety.
- **Microclimate:** The localized environmental conditions around the plant, such as temperature, sunlight, and wind, which influence growth.
- **Black Spot:** A common fungal disease that causes black spots on leaves, often leading to defoliation if untreated.
- **Cane:** A main stem or branch of a rose bush, which supports leaves, buds, and flowers.
- **Overwintering:** The care and protection provided to miniature roses during the cold months to prevent frost damage and ensure healthy growth in spring.

Troubleshooting List

Quick Reference Guide for Common Problems

1. **Yellowing Leaves**

   - **Causes**: Nutrient deficiencies, poor drainage, overwatering, pest infestations.
   - **Solutions**: Fertilize properly, improve soil drainage, monitor and manage pests regularly.

2. **Black Spot**

   - **Causes**: Fungal disease causing black spots and yellowing leaves; thrives in warm, humid conditions.
   - **Solutions**: Provide proper spacing for air circulation, avoid overhead watering, apply fungicides regularly, remove and dispose of affected leaves.

3. **Powdery Mildew**

   - **Causes**: White, powdery coating on leaves, stems, and buds; favored by dry, warm conditions with poor air circulation.
   - **Solutions**: Increase air flow around plants, maintain consistent soil moisture, use fungicides as needed, prune to improve air circulation.

4. **Aphids**

   - **Causes**: Small, sap-sucking insects found on new growth and buds.

- **Solutions**: Introduce beneficial insects like ladybugs, use insecticidal soap, regularly inspect plants, dislodge with strong water sprays.

5. **Spider Mites**

    - **Causes**: Tiny pests causing stippling and yellowing of leaves; thrive in hot, dry conditions.
    - **Solutions**: Regularly mist plants, use miticides, encourage natural predators, ensure adequate humidity.

6. **Root Rot**

    - **Causes**: Waterlogged soil leading to rotting roots.
    - **Solutions**: Improve soil drainage, avoid overwatering, use well-draining soil mixes, remove affected plants and treat the soil.

7. **Poor Bloom Production**

    - **Causes**: Insufficient light, inadequate fertilization, improper pruning.
    - Solutions: Ensure at least six hours of direct sunlight daily, apply balanced fertilizers, follow proper pruning practices, regular maintenance and monitoring.

Miniature Rose Care Checklist

Daily Tasks

1. Check for pests and diseases.
2. Monitor soil moisture.
3. Inspect plants for signs of stress or nutrient deficiencies.

Weekly Tasks

1. Water deeply and thoroughly.
2. Apply balanced, water-soluble fertilizer.
3. Deadhead spent flowers.
4. Weed the garden bed.
5. Inspect for signs of stress or nutrient deficiencies.

Monthly Tasks

1. Perform light pruning to maintain plant shape.
2. Replenish mulch around the base of plants.
3. Conduct soil tests for nutrient levels and pH.
4. Apply organic amendments as needed.

Seasonal Tasks

1. **Spring**
    - Plant new roses and perform major pruning.
    - Apply slow-release fertilizer.
    - Check and repair irrigation systems.
2. **Summer**
    - Maintain consistent watering and pest management.
    - Deadhead regularly.
    - Provide shade during the hottest part of the day.
    - Ensure adequate hydration.
3. **Autumn**
    - Prepare roses for dormancy by reducing watering and fertilization.
    - Clean up fallen leaves and debris.
    - Light pruning to shape plants.
    - Apply a thick layer of mulch.
4. **Winter**
    - Protect roses from extreme cold.
    - Maintain mulch layer and consider additional insulation.
    - Minimal pruning to avoid stimulating growth.
    - Monitor for signs of damage or disease.

Conclusion

Recap of Key Points

Throughout this comprehensive guide, we have explored various aspects of growing and caring for miniature roses. Starting with an understanding of soil health and fertility, we delved into organic amendments, composting, and soil testing. These foundational practices support robust growth and blooming. We then examined companion planting and biodiversity, highlighting beneficial companion plants, creating a balanced ecosystem, and using pest-repellent plants to enhance garden health.

Sustainable and eco-friendly practices, such as reducing chemical use, water conservation techniques, and encouraging wildlife, were discussed to promote a healthier garden environment. These practices help maintain a balanced ecosystem and reduce the environmental impact of gardening. We also provided a glossary of essential terms for rose gardeners, a troubleshooting list for common problems, and a detailed care checklist outlining daily, weekly, monthly, and seasonal tasks.

Encouragement for Your Gardening Journey

Embarking on the journey of growing miniature roses can be both rewarding and challenging. With patience, dedication, and the knowledge gained from this guide, gardeners can cultivate beautiful and healthy rose plants. Each step, from soil preparation to daily maintenance, contributes to the success and enjoyment of rose gardening. Embrace the learning process, and don't be discouraged by setbacks. Every challenge encountered is an opportunity to grow and improve as a gardener.

Printed in Dunstable, United Kingdom